More Praise for *Thriving in the Second C*

"Behind every good lead pastor, there is an equall-
often shoulders the same responsibility without tl
be tricky to navigate, and if you get it wrong, the c
want your church to grow, you must invest in this …nd
Thriving in the Second Chair to any pastor or director … a lead pastor."
—Matt Miofsky, Lead Pastor, The Gathering (UMC), … Louis, MO

"A good leader knows that all of us are smarter than any one of us and that we can do more and better work together than we can alone. The question is, how? In *Thriving in the Second Chair,* Mike Bonem answers that question. Leaders at every level of an organization will benefit from this book. If you seek to maximize your working relationship in a way that produces greater results for your team, this book is for you."
—Tom Billings, Executive Director, Union Baptist Association

"This book is both imminently readable and practical. With a great balance of challenging ideas, Mike weaves in real-life stories of ministry. He shows the vibrancy of the partnership between Senior and Executive Pastors. This is a must-read for all in the second chair."
—David Fletcher, founder of XPastor and Executive Pastor of First EvFree Fullerton, Fullerton, CA

"The impact of a business or ministry is directly tied to the relational health of its leadership team. Where disunity or unclear communication exist, missions are likely to drift off course. *Thriving in the Second Chair* is a compelling, clear, and practical guide that will equip leaders for more effective service. Mike helps align vision, strengthen collaboration, and deepen trust-based relationships. For teams seeking to make a significant impact, I highly recommend this book!"
—Peter Greer, president and CEO of HOPE International; coauthor of *Mission Drift*

"As one who has spent almost forty years as a second chair leader in ministry, I encourage you to work through *Thriving in the Second Chair.* This engaging resource leads you through ten springs of fresh water for the journey. It is real world and practical. Every second chair leader will recognize the journey and shout 'me too.'"
—Phill Martin, Deputy CEO, The Church Network

"Mike's first book for second chair leaders had a foundational impact on me as a leader. This new work is an entirely different perspective on that pivotal role. Taking a more personal approach, Mike gives us real tools for thriving in the midst of the ups and downs of ministry life. All second chair leaders need to move this to the very top of their reading list."
—Phil Taylor, Executive Pastor of Leadership and Development, Mosaic Church in Winter Garden & Walt Disney World; author of *Defining the Executive Pastor Role*

"Mike Bonem continually 'hits the nail on the head' regarding the complex realities of church leadership. This book ought to be on every second chair's reading list, second only to the Bible. It will help you thrive in that zone between clarity and flexibility, between chaos and order. I wish this book had been available when I began leading from the second chair over a decade ago!"
—Bob Johnson, Executive Pastor, Chapelwood United Methodist Church, Houston, TX

"Mike Bonem's writing has been an invaluable source of wisdom for me in my roles as an executive leader in two large multi-site churches. *Leading from the Second Chair* was a lifeline in my early days of ministry leadership, and I continue to recommend it to every second chair leader I know. In *Thriving in the Second Chair*, Mike addresses the sincere challenges that second chair leaders face and equips you with the tools to not just survive but thrive."
—Jenni Catron, CEO of The 4Sight Group and author of *The 4 Dimensions of Extraordinary Leadership*

"*Thriving in the Second Chair* is a 'must-read' for senior pastors and their associates, bishops and their cabinets, and executive church leaders and their staff. Grounded in deep spiritual truths and honest conversation, *Thriving* offers sensible, thoughtful pathways for leadership teams to flourish in their work on behalf of God's mission. Bonem is superb at honoring individual uniqueness while helping the organization focus on its mission. *Thriving* is a marvelous tool to plumb deep springs of conversation among the church's leaders."
—Janice Riggle Huie, retired Bishop of The Texas Annual Conference (UMC)

"He did it. Again. Somehow Mike Bonem crawled back into the minds of second chair leaders and translated our thoughts, concerns, insights, fears, joys, and experiences into a much-needed book. Mike continues to challenge every second chair to live up to God's calling for our very unique positions. Not only should every second chair read this book but every first chair should as well. Thriving brings clarity to how leaders can work together to further the Kingdom in an awe-inspiring, God-honoring, community-transforming way."
—Judy West, Pastor/Staff & Leadership Development, The Crossing, St. Louis

"A few pages into this book, I realized that it is for all of us who navigate the challenging waters of a second chair role! It provides thoughtful insights for leaders at every level who aren't willing to simply survive but who truly desire to thrive."
—Jon Ferguson, Founding Pastor of Community Christian Church and Movement Leader of NewThing Network

THRIVING *in the* SECOND CHAIR

Linda,
I'm grateful for the ways that
you've helped me to thrive and
I'm praying that you will thrive
like a tree planted by streams
of water (Psalm 1:3).
Mike

Other Books by the Author

In Pursuit of Great AND *Godly Leadership*

Leading from the Second Chair (with Roger Patterson)

Leading Congregational Change (with Jim Herrington and James Furr)

THRIVING *in the* SECOND CHAIR

Ten Practices for Robust Ministry
(When You're Not in Charge)

MIKE BONEM

Nashville

THRIVING IN THE SECOND CHAIR:
TEN PRACTICES FOR ROBUST MINISTRY (WHEN YOU'RE NOT IN CHARGE)

Library of Congress Cataloging-in-Publication Data has been requested.

ISBN 978-1-5018-1424-2

16 17 18 19 20 21 22 23 24 25—10 9 8 7 6 5 4 3 2 1

MANUFACTURED IN THE UNITED STATES OF AMERICA

To Jim Turley
Friend, encourager, pastor, servant, and man of prayer. Thanks for always seeing the best in me and praying toward that end. My journey is far richer because God allowed our paths to intersect.

And to the many other friends that I've made through TMF. You will never know how much I have grown and been blessed through your presence in my life.

Contents

Acknowledgments

This is the space where I'm supposed to name all the different people who have contributed to this project. It's an impossible task, because this book has been shaped by so many second chair leaders. They've invited me into their lives as a coach or friend. I've had one-time conversations with some, while other relationships have spanned many years. Their stories appear throughout this book and have shaped my understanding of the ten practices for thriving. I won't try to name them all because there's not enough room (and because I would inevitably forget someone). So let me start by expressing my appreciation to each of the second chairs who have crossed my path and enriched my journey over the past decade.

In the same way, I can't name all of the people for whom I'm grateful at West University Baptist and Crosspoint Church, where I was a second chair leader for eleven years. They allowed me to lead and to learn, to be a pastor and a friend. Thanks to Barry Landrum and Roger Patterson, the two senior pastors I served, and many other friends on the staff for the ways that they encouraged and supported me.

The Leadership Ministry of Texas Methodist Foundation (TMF) has blessed me with the opportunity to facilitate learning communities for second chair leaders. Thanks to Tom Locke, Jim Turley, and Lisa Greenwood for making this possible, and to each member of these groups for being living examples of the practices for thriving and helping me to thrive in the process. Even though the TMF groups are just mentioned at one place in the body of this book, their influence flows throughout.

Writing may sound like a solitary endeavor, but it's not a solo effort to produce a book. It has been an absolute delight to work with Constance Stella and the rest of the team at Abingdon. The final product is better in every respect because of the ways they have nurtured this project. I'm also grateful to Tom Billings, Bob Johnson, and Judy West who offered tremendous insights, input, and encouragement on the first draft of the manuscript.

My biggest supporters are my family, and I owe them my greatest appreciation. Bonnie is the love of my life, my best friend, and my greatest champion, and I couldn't have completed this book without her. Thanks also to our children—David and Karlie, Matthew, Jonathan and Kellie, and Hope—for the time that I took away from them so that I could write; and to my parents, Joe and Diane, for always believing in me.

Finally, I thank God for the abilities and opportunities that he has given me. My prayer is that this project reflects good stewardship of those gifts, that it will bear fruit for the Kingdom, and that God will be glorified as a result.

Introduction

Beyond Leading

I have no doubt that you are leading from the second chair, but are you thriving? Over the past decade, I've become convinced that this is a pivotal question for second chair leaders. It's the question that can explain the difference between leadership that is filled with grace and joy versus labored frustration. It affects how long second chair leaders remain in the role. It spills over into all of their relationships. Unfortunately, many second chair leaders would answer that they are just surviving, not thriving.

When Roger Patterson and I wrote *Leading from the Second Chair*, we said that it was the start of a conversation about how to be effective in this vital ministry role. And indeed, I've had countless conversations since then. Those conversations have been with men and women, rookie and long-tenured second chairs, individuals who have spent their entire careers in ministry and others who excelled in business before stepping into a ministry role. They have been in large and mid-size churches, denominational bodies, compassion agencies, mission-sending organizations, and a variety of other ministries. Some have been deeply satisfied in their work, while others have endured seasons in which they struggled. They have had a variety of titles, but the common denominator is that each has been "a person in a subordinate role whose influence with others adds value throughout the entire organization."[1]

Along the way, I've become convinced that it's not enough to lead from the second chair. Second chair leaders need to thrive, not just survive. They

1. Mike Bonem and Roger Patterson, *Leading from the Second Chair: Serving Your Church, Fulfilling Your Role, and Realizing Your Dreams* (San Francisco: Jossey-Bass, 2005), 2. See appendix A of this book for an overview of the key concepts from *Leading from the Second Chair.*

need to thrive not only for their own well-being but also for the benefit of the church or ministry they serve. If leading from the second chair is a vital ingredient to organizational success, thriving enables them to lead with enthusiasm and joy.

You may think that external factors determine whether you will thrive. I won't deny the significance of your context, but it's too easy—and inaccurate—to place all the blame on uncontrollable outside forces. If you truly want to thrive, your hands are not tied behind your back. There are steps you can take.

In the early stages of their wilderness wandering, the Israelite people weren't thriving. At times they didn't even think they would survive. They grumbled about their circumstances. They cried out because they were afraid that they would die in the desert for lack of water. But God was with them the entire time. He knew their needs and how to quench their thirst, whether by leading them to an oasis (Exod 15:27) or to a rock that would produce all the water they needed (Exod 17:5-7). The water was there all along—they just needed to trust God and be led to it. God didn't change the external realities but rather helped them discover something they didn't know.

This story is applicable for second chair leaders. The difference between surviving and thriving is like two people who are wandering in a desert, one with only a canteen and the other who knows the location of every stream and spring. The conditions in the desert are harsh for both of them. The risks are always present. But the one who knows where to find water can live—and even thrive—in the desert indefinitely.

My goal in writing this book is simple. I want to give you a map of the "springs" that enable second chair leaders to thrive. The map comes from my own journey in this role and the countless conversations that I've had with other second chair leaders. It highlights the places that will help you do more than survive. It points beyond external circumstances to the ways that you can act and think differently. To borrow from another well-known image in Scripture, I want you to know where and how the Good Shepherd can lead you beside still waters.

As I've looked at (and lived in) the complex landscape of second chair leadership, I've discovered ten deep springs. "Deep" is important. In the same way that a shallow spring may dry up in times of drought, some factors that bring satisfaction to second chair leaders are not reliable or long-lasting. I want to lead you to springs that you can count on, even in a drought. What are the practices associated with these deep springs?

Growing toward a partnership with your first chair where trust and shared decision-making are the norm. A true partnership can take years to achieve, but thriving second chair leaders do their part to move in that direction.

Living with, and helping to lift, the "lids" that limit your first chair's leadership. Every leader has room for improvement. Thriving second chairs seek to be catalysts for their first chair's growth while remaining patient with the weaknesses.

Clarifying your role as much as possible. Second chairs know that there will always be ambiguity in their roles, so they thrive by living in the balance between pursuing clarity and demonstrating flexibility.

Thinking and acting strategically to keep the church or ministry focused on the most important priorities. Second chair leaders who thrive add great value by seeing the big picture and making decisions in light of this.

Developing staff with a future-oriented perspective. Those who thrive view "supervision" as an opportunity to coach and develop staff members toward success, even when facing difficult situations.

Organizing selectively to bring order to chaos. A thriving second chair resists the temptation to organize everything and focuses on the places where structure is most needed and valuable.

Navigating governance nuances as they relate to boards and committees. Thriving second chairs don't overstep their boundaries but navigate this delicate dance in ways that advance the mission, support the first chair, and maintain unity.

Staying spiritually anchored for identity and affirmation. The second chair role can seem thankless and invisible. Those who thrive don't depend on affirmation from their first chair, other leaders, or tangible accomplishments because their identity is anchored in Christ.

Overcoming loneliness by sharing your journey with trusted peers. Second chair leaders often feel isolated even though they are surrounded by people. Forming safe relationships for camaraderie and wise counsel is essential for thriving.

Extending your shelf life by reinventing your role. Stagnation is a real danger that can cause second chairs to leave. Reinventing the role offers a way for them to thrive and be reenergized.

The first three springs relate to the single most important professional relationship for any second chair leader—their relationship with the first chair. The next four look at some of the most common and essential aspects of the second chair's job. Even though there are many different kinds of second chair leaders, these springs will quench the thirst that is experienced in a variety of positions.

Much of the content related to these first seven springs focuses on things that second chairs can, and should, do to improve their context. In essence, they provide practical suggestions to the person who says, "How can I make this second chair role more enjoyable and fulfilling?" The final three springs are arguably the deepest and most important. They enable second chairs to thrive even if they're struggling with the first seven. These offer hope to the person who wonders, "Is it possible to thrive even when I'm having trouble finding water from the other sources?"

The ten springs for thriving are relatively independent of each other. While I believe that each is important, you will undoubtedly be drawn to some more than others. You may already be familiar with one or think that another isn't applicable for you. This book is written so that you can skip chapters or read in whatever order you choose.

It is also written for more than second chair leaders in churches and ministries. While that is certainly the book's primary audience, many of the practices for thriving are applicable for any ministry leader and even Christian leaders who work in secular settings. Even if you don't see yourself as a person who "adds value throughout the organization," it is important for you to thrive.

As you thought about the brief descriptions of the ten springs for thriving, you may have nodded your head. Perhaps you recognized one or more areas where you are thriving. If so, let me encourage you to stop right now and offer a prayer of thanksgiving.

In other cases, you may have paused when you saw a vital element that is missing in your life. If that's the case, you may not have nodded in affirmation. Instead, a few wrinkles may have appeared on your forehead as you expressed a central question: "How? How can I find these springs that will enable me to thrive?" That is the question that drove me to write this book. If you're interested in the answer, join the continuation of the second chair conversation on the pages that follow.

Chapter 1

Grow toward Partnership

A true partnership can take years to achieve, but thriving second chair leaders do their part to move in that direction.

Partnership. I don't think I've ever met a second chair leader who didn't desire to be in an effective partnership with his or her first chair. Second chair leaders know that a partnership makes it possible for their church or ministry to soar and for them to experience greater fulfillment in their roles. In the eyes of many second chairs, a partnership is the pot of gold at the end of the leadership rainbow.

Most first chair leaders also endorse the value and power of a partnership. They know that the task of leading their church or ministry toward its mission is daunting and is more than any one person can accomplish. They would welcome a trusted co-laborer who can help shoulder this heavy burden.

And yet, partnerships remain elusive for most first and second chairs. This gap between aspiration and reality occurs in all different kinds of organizations: churches and denominational bodies and parachurch ministries of all different sizes, ones with well-defined visions and ones that struggle with setting clear direction. The gap can occur whether the leadership team is composed of two people or more. It can even occur when first and second chairs both desire a partnership and have years of experience working together.

Why? If a partnership is so valuable, and if everyone desires to have one, why do so many leadership teams fall short of this gold standard?

It Starts with a Definition

Many potential partnerships never get off the ground because the leaders don't work from a shared definition. If the first and second chairs talk about working as partners but have fundamentally different ideas of what this means, tension is guaranteed and "partnership" will be nothing more than lip service.

So what is a partnership? My definition is:

> A commitment to sharing directional leadership decisions that is based on a common vision, an appreciation for each other's complementary gifts, and a high level of trust that develops over time.

In light of this definition, where do potential partnerships get off track? The most notable struggle for second chairs is when they interpret partnership to mean equality. Notice that this definition does not say that the parties are "equals" on the organization chart or that they have the same title (e.g., co-pastor). It does not imply that they both answer to the governing body. While there are some partnerships that operate in this manner, these are the rare exceptions. There are many effective partnerships in which it is clear that one person is the boss.

Most first chair leaders presume some amount of inequality in the relationship. Regardless of how often partnership terminology is used, first chairs feel the weight of responsibility for the church or ministry's success or failure. Their definition often goes askew when they think of the second chair as a "junior partner." This connotation sounds like a large law firm that may have many "partners." In these firms, only a few of the partners actually have leadership responsibility for the firm. The other partners have a title and significant responsibility, but they don't meet the definition offered above.

Like those law firm partners, second chair leaders may carry heavy leadership loads. The first chair may think of them as "partners in ministry." They may even be on the senior leadership team or serve as a member of the organization's governing body. They can do all of these things and add great value for the organization, but fall short of being a partner as defined above.

When a true partnership is found, it has almost always developed over time. Darlene[1] had served for over a decade in a second chair role in her church, but she would say that she had only been a true partner for two years. She had always

1. The names throughout this book are fictitious, but the stories are based on real second chair leaders.

made a substantial leadership contribution, overseeing key initiatives, and managing much of the staff. The shift to being a partner was subtle, never official, and without a change in title. It began when Carl, the senior pastor, asked Darlene to help him lead a strategic planning process. He then asked her to spearhead the capital campaign that followed. But just as meaningful were the ways that he sought her advice more often on important issues, gave her a broader range of responsibilities, and rarely looked over her shoulder.

If you find yourself yearning to be in a true partnership, start by examining your own definition of what that means. If you have an expectation of being co-leaders, it may be time to recalibrate your expectations. Once you've done the hard work of self-examination, then you're ready for a discussion with your first chair about his or her understanding of what partnership means, how a partnership can strengthen your church or ministry, and what steps you can take to move toward one.

The Benefits of a Partnership

Even if there is agreement on the definition of partnership, first chairs may be reluctant to embrace this model. Why? Because they are not convinced that the benefits outweigh the risks.

You may wonder, "What risks?" But consider the first chair's perspective. "Sharing directional leadership decisions" requires releasing a great deal of control and authority. It creates the possibility of disagreement that can't be resolved with the first chair trump card: "Because I said so." It requires more time for making decisions. It introduces a new wrinkle in how accountability plays out, both with the partner and with the governing body. From a first chair's viewpoint, a partnership can look quite risky.

That's why it is important to clearly see the benefits. On the heels of a discussion about the definition of partnership, first and second chair leaders should articulate the advantages of this arrangement. While there are many benefits from a high-capacity person serving in the second chair, four relate uniquely to having a true partner:

- Better decisions. No one, regardless of the chair they occupy or their experience or their intellectual prowess, has all the information needed to make great strategic decisions every time. A partner brings different information, knowledge, and perspective to the table. Of course, nonpartners can also offer this value, but the commitment to shared decision-making in a partnership means that the alternative perspective can't be ignored.

- Higher buy-in. There is a noticeable difference in the energy level of second chair leaders who are treated as partners. They shift from talking about decisions in second or third person language (your priorities or his or her priorities) to first person plural (our priorities). This is far deeper than a shift in language. It indicates a level of ownership and commitment that helps propel the church or ministry forward.

- Accelerate the mission. It's no surprise, then, that the combination of better decisions and higher buy-in can have a huge impact on the trajectory of the organization. When two (or three) leaders are on the same page and are deeply committed to the mission, great outcomes are possible, and they become possible more quickly.

- Beyond loyalty. Every first chair wants the rest of the staff to be loyal. This generally is understood to mean not undermining his or her authority and diligently performing work that has been assigned. But when second chairs are partners, loyalty should not even be a question. That's because they think of "our decisions" and "our organization." If there's a problem, it is "our problem," not something to be blamed on the first chair.

As you read through these benefits, you may think that I'm preaching to the choir. In your second chair role, you see all of the advantages of a partnership, including some that I've not even mentioned. But have you discussed these with your first chair leader?

The Foundation for a Partnership

Those initial conversations between first and second chairs about the definition and benefits of partnership are important, but they are only the beginning. You cannot live into the ideal of sharing directional leadership decisions if you don't lay the foundation that is described in the rest of the definition: *a common vision, an appreciation for each other's complementary gifts, and a high level of trust that develops over time.*

Common Vision

It's impossible to share directional leadership decisions without a shared vision. I know that the "V" word can be confusing because it has been used in many different ways. I define vision as the "clear, shared, and compelling description of God's preferred future for your church or ministry."[2] It describes where God is leading, and in doing so, begins to set priorities for your church or ministry.

Having a common vision does not mean that first and second chairs are always in agreement on how to achieve that vision. That's where the hard work of shared decision-making comes in. Nor does it mean that both leaders need to be "visionaries." In fact, having multiple visionary leaders is often a recipe for disaster. A common vision does, however, mean that each partner is excited about the same big dreams for the church or ministry.

Imagine a senior pastor whose eyes sparkle and voice changes when he talks about a network of mission partnerships in Africa. It is clear that this is a central part of his vision. If you're sitting in the second chair and thinking, *Yes, but what about the needs in our community or in our own congregation?* that may be a warning sign that common vision is lacking. On the other hand, you may feel your own excitement level rising as you hear your senior pastor talk about this vision. You may still have questions: How many partnerships? What will they look like? Can we afford this? But questions about strategy and implementation are not a sign of divergent visions. (See chapter 4 for more on strategy.)

This illustration is not meant to suggest that first chair leaders have exclusive rights in determining organizational vision. In the most effective organizations, first and second chairs (as well as other leaders) come together to discern God's preferred future for their church or ministry. They may discover a "both/and" vision that includes global and local missions. But it will never work to have the "partners" pursuing separate visions. A successful partnership must be built on a common vision.

Appreciation for Complementary Gifts

One of the great benefits of a partnership is the fact that a second chair brings different gifts, experiences, and perspectives to the leadership table. One of the great tensions for many first–second chair relationships is the fact that a second chair brings different gifts, experiences, and perspectives to the table. The

2. Jim Herrington, Mike Bonem, and James Furr, *Leading Congregational Change: A Practical Guide for the Transformational Journey* (San Francisco: Jossey-Bass, 2000), 50.

very things that can make a leadership team stronger can also tear at the fabric of unity that is essential for their effectiveness.

The visionary pastor dreams about a network of mission partnerships in Africa. His dreams are full of energy and passion, which builds excitement and commitment in the congregation. The executive pastor is much more "practical." He can't help but think about the details. And there are plenty of details to work out to make this dream a reality.

In relationships that struggle, these different gifts are often seen as weaknesses or "problems." The executive pastor rolls his eyes and thinks, *My senior pastor has never met an idea that he didn't like* or, *He has no idea what he's committing us to do.* The senior pastor sees a flash of exasperation on the face of the executive pastor and thinks, *There he goes again. I've never had a dream that he couldn't kill in less than five minutes.*

In great partnerships, the diversity of gifts may be considerable. What is different in these relationships is that the partners value each other's unique strengths. The executive pastor knows that he is neither visionary nor charismatic, and that the church has done many bold things for God through the senior pastor's leadership. The senior pastor knows that the executive pastor has kept him (and the church) from rushing off of more than one cliff and has a tremendous ability to take raw ideas and turn them into reality. Appreciation for complementary gifts may not always be easy, but it is essential in a true partnership.

High Level of Trust

Common vision and appreciation for complementary gifts are important, but trust is the bedrock of a healthy partnership. Just as in a marriage, there will be both good and difficult times in the relationship between first and second chairs. Trust is the factor that will sustain the relationship in those rough patches.

In *The Five Dysfunctions of a Team*, leadership expert Patrick Lencioni puts "building trust" at the base of the pyramid for overcoming unhealthy team dynamics.[3] When trust levels are high, team members are willing to talk through their differences. They are more likely to think the best of each other and to give the benefit of the doubt. When trust is low, even small disagreements can spiral out of control as colleagues question each other's intentions.

3. Patrick Lencioni, *The Five Dysfunctions of a Team: A Leadership Fable* (San Francisco: Jossey-Bass, 2002), 188.

The senior pastor with a passion for missions in Africa faces an important question when his executive pastor starts asking about details that he hasn't considered. In that moment, will he *trust* that the executive pastor's intent is good? Will he believe that the executive pastor is only asking out of love for the church and the senior pastor? Or will the senior pastor hear these as "pesky" questions? Will he become suspicious, wondering what's behind the questions and suspecting that the executive pastor is undermining him? His mind could go either way in an instant, without even consciously processing these reactions. The difference in the two scenarios has little to do with the specifics of the moment and everything to do with how much trust has been built in the relationship.

If you want to thrive in the second chair, and if you aspire to a true partnership with your first chair leader, start by building trust. Don't make the mistake of thinking that trust is primarily performance based. It is important that you do a good job and that you follow through on any commitments you've made. In those cases, your first chair may say, "I trust her to do a good job." This may result in a commendation or increased responsibility, but great performance alone doesn't lead to a partnership.

True partnerships are anchored in relationship-based trust. It's the confidence that the partners have each other's backs. It's a track record of supporting one another. It's an ability to disagree without destroying the relationship. This trust requires being quick to apologize for mistakes and being equally quick to forgive. Those who fully trust have learned to keep short accounts with each other. They don't sweep things under the rug. They either forget about a grievance, or they deal with it in God-honoring ways.

Perhaps I'm preaching to the choir again, so let me ask a simple question: Do you have this kind of trust with your first chair leader? Does he or she trust you in the ways described above? If not, why not? What can you do to build trust?

Over Time

All of the foundational elements for a partnership, especially trust, take time. Over the years, I have interacted with many highly capable second chair leaders. They have consistently described a period of three to five years before they were performing at their full capacity.

At first, these responses didn't make sense to me. These people were generally gifted leaders before they stepped into the second chair. But on further reflection, I realized that they were describing the length of time before they functioned as true partners. Their learning curve was less about the skills to do the job than the nuances of the relationship. Partnerships are built on trust, and trust cannot be microwaved. Just like in a marriage, you can do a number of things along the way to make it great, but you can't rush the final product.

If you're feeling frustrated that you're not a true partner, how long have you been in your role? If your answer is less than three years, are you experiencing growth in the relationship that is moving you toward a partnership? It's possible that you simply need to be patient.

Can You Dance with More than Two?

I vividly remember one second chair's comment when I asked him about the transition to a new senior pastor: "We're still learning how to dance together." It's a great image for any second chair to keep in mind. Dancing has an element that is technical and mechanical—following the beat of the music, knowing the steps of the dance. But if this is all that you master, the dance will not have any beauty. When two people dance well together, they transcend the technical aspects. There's grace in their moves. They anticipate each other's actions. They can be spontaneous and well coordinated at the same time.

This raises a natural question: Is it possible to have an effective partnership with more than two people? Can you still create a beautiful, fluid leadership dance with three or four people? Just as in a dance, the complexity grows exponentially with each additional person, but it is possible to create a strong leadership team that has the characteristics of partnership described in the preceding section.

Most large churches and ministries have a leadership or executive team. That group may or may not function as a true partnership. The ones that do tend to be smaller (three or four people rather than six or eight) and they truly share directional leadership decisions. They are more likely to have a spirited conversation that ends in consensus rather than a debate with the first chair making the final decision. They rely on the different gifts that each person brings to the table. They value the unity of the team above almost anything else.

Alan, the executive director of a large compassion ministry, has three associate directors who report to him. While each has a specific area of responsibility, they all bring the big-picture perspective to their team meetings. Their long tenure together has enabled them to build a high level of trust so that they can have healthy disagreements on strategic issues and even raise questions about issues in a colleague's area of ministry. Even though Alan has the authority and credibility to insist on a certain course of action, he rarely uses this power. Instead, the four members of this team sit as (near) equals in strategic discussions and look to reach a consensus as often as possible. They find that they must work hard at communication and resolving conflict, but they have learned to dance well together.

Another variation is to have a partnership that is a subset within a larger leadership team. In this case, the bigger group will be involved in the major directional decisions. The various members will bring different perspectives and will give input. They will typically have important responsibilities within the organization. But only the individual second chair leader truly functions as a partner with the first chair.

You may find that you're on a leadership team that is frustrated because you're not dancing well together. You, or others on the team, may be expecting a partnership that's not in the cards. Your next step may be to spend time within the team discussing your collective purpose and each member's expectations.

What If the First Chair Doesn't Dance?

Partnerships with more than two people can be complex, but the bigger challenge is when the first chair resists having a partnership with anyone. You know the old expression "It takes two to tango." You can try to start the music by talking about the benefits of a partnership, but if you drag an unwilling first chair leader onto the dance floor, the result will be anything but beautiful.

Up to this point, we've focused on understanding what a true partnership looks like, but many second chair leaders are not invited into a partnership relationship. If this describes you, what should you do? Is the only other option to wait for orders from the commander-in-chief?

Fortunately, it's not this black and white. If a true partnership is the ideal relationship between first and second chairs, the opposite is a heavy-handed, hierarchical leadership style. But there are many points on a continuum between these two extremes. For example, a ministry's executive director may willingly and genuinely listen to input from a second chair but consistently reserve the decision-making authority for herself. It's not quite a partnership, as defined above, but this is a second chair role with a high degree of influence. Or a second chair may be given some broad strategic boundaries by her boss, and then be given a relatively free hand to lead and act within that context.

Luke is serving as Chris's second chair for the second time in his career. They served together at a previous church, and after Chris moved to his current, larger church, he soon asked Luke to join him. Luke's responsibilities include supervising much of the staff, preaching regularly in one of the worship services, and helping to set the church's strategic priorities. But if you asked Luke to evaluate his role against the definition of "partnership," he would be quick to tell you that it falls short of this standard. Luke is a valued lieutenant, but his relationship with Chris lacks the level of trust and the shared decision-making that characterizes a partnership. He is closer to the partner side of the continuum but not at the far end.

Where are you on this continuum? In a true partnership, the distance between first and second chairs feels as though it's only a millimeter. When you're working for a demanding, top-down leader, you feel a mile apart, regardless of your title or responsibilities. What is the distance for you?

More importantly, regardless of where you are on this continuum, what practical steps can you take to shrink the distance? Many of these steps are embedded in the definition of a true partnership, but they deserve further comment from the perspective of a second chair who wants to shrink the distance so that it's closer to one millimeter.

Earn trust. Trust is not only essential in a partnership; it is the key ingredient to shift toward that ideal. From a first chair's perspective, trust and loyalty are inseparable. Simply stated, a second chair who is not perceived as loyal won't be trusted. Loyalty is far more than abstaining from direct attacks on the first chair. It is evident in conversations (when the first chair is present and absent), in tone of voice, and in body language.

Being loyal, however, does not mean that a second chair can't disagree. The most effective second chairs are leaders, and leaders will have strong ideas at times. Trustworthy second chairs know how to disagree respectfully, often behind closed doors, and always assessing whether the issue at hand is important enough to merit the challenge. When a first chair leader believes that a second chair is loyal, feels respected by the second chair, and knows that disagreements are chosen judiciously, it creates the potential for greater trust.

Strive for excellence. First chair leaders also expect to see a high level of competence from their second chairs. Moving along the continuum toward a partnership almost always involves increasing levels of responsibility and autonomy. If a second chair has not performed with excellence in whatever duties may have been assigned, the first chair will be reluctant to expand the role.

It really doesn't matter what the specific duties are. They may relate to a special project or supervising a difficult staff member or interfacing with a key committee. They may be a central part of the second chair's role or just one of the "other duties as may be assigned" that is written at the end of virtually every job description. If these tasks are not done well, the first chair will question whether the second chair is ready for more.

If you want to grow as a second chair, take Colossians 3:23 to heart: "Work at it with all your heart, as working for the Lord." Let your first chair see that you tackle any task with diligence and that you get things done. If there are reasons why you can't do it well—perhaps you have too much on your plate, or you're being asked to do something that is far outside of your gifting—brainstorm with your first chair early to identify other solutions. Don't let it be said that you are someone who is just getting by.

Own your mistakes. So what happens when the end result isn't excellent? Second chair leaders who want to grow toward a partnership own their mistakes. Good leaders know that success is not guaranteed and that some failures will occur in any church or ministry that is attempting to follow a God-sized vision. First chairs are concerned about missteps, but they are much more concerned if a second chair leader doesn't accept and learn from them.

A growing amount of leadership literature describes the value of hiring people who have experienced failure. It has become common in corporate interviews to ask a leadership candidate to describe a time when he failed, how he handled that failure, and what he learned from it. Think of your desire to move further along the continuum as an "interview." When things don't go right, how do you handle them and what do you learn? These questions will shape your first chair's perception of your readiness to be a partner.

Forgive their mistakes (quickly). Forgiveness is at the heart of the Christian faith, and it's at the heart of healthy partnerships. It's impossible to have a close working relationship in which major decisions are being made without having moments of tension or disagreement. Your first chair will hurt or offend you at times.

Some second chairs think that they can't talk to their first chair about this. After all, the first chair is the boss. And so these second chairs often choose to harbor frustration or resentment rather than addressing an issue. Not only is this not biblical, it will eventually impact the relationship. The gap between the two of you will grow if tension is left unaddressed. Future slights will be magnified. You'll become more critical or skeptical of your first chair's decisions.

It's far better to keep short accounts. If an issue needs to be addressed, then do so. And whether it's addressed or not, forgive your first chair. Know that they are imperfect and that you are too. By offering forgiveness wholly and quickly, you put yourself in a position to be the beneficiary of the same in the future.

Clarify the vision. True partnership is impossible without a common vision. It's a relatively easy decision to leave if you realize that your vision doesn't align with that of the first chair and the church or ministry. All of the other leadership decisions should be driven by the vision. If it's not shared, conflict is inevitable.

But what if the vision is murky? In those cases, second chairs will regularly find the first chair asking, "Why did you do that?" This is a sign that the second chair's action was based on an incorrect interpretation of the vision.

Rather than treating this moment as a failure or a rebuke, it should be seen as an opportunity for clarification. Start by rethinking the decision or action in your own mind. Why did it seem appropriate based on your understanding of the vision? Then explain this to your first chair, and end with a question: "Can you help me understand where I went wrong? What would you have done in this situation? And why?"

When Erin launched the first satellite campus for her church, she was given very little direction other than to "reach the community with the gospel." She knew that the church's culture encouraged risk-taking and rewarded leaders who got results. The campus far exceeded everyone's expectations in its first two years, so Erin was surprised to feel a tightening of the reins—more coordination of sermons, vetting of mission projects by the mission department at the "main" campus, approvals for hiring new staff members. Erin had assumed that effectively reaching the community was the highest value. In further discussions with her senior pastor, she learned that this was a priority, but the value of acting as "one church in multiple locations" was equally important. The conversations simply brought clarity to the vision.

Demonstrate that you care. The second chair is a difficult, and often lonely, role. (More on loneliness in chapter 9.) But the same can be said of the first chair. The weight of leadership, knowing that the buck stops on their desk, weighs heavily on the shoulders of almost every pastor or other first chair leader. They are surrounded by people, and yet they carry these burdens in isolation. They often lack deep relationships with peers. The volunteers who are their closest advisors don't really understand all that the first chair job entails.

That places second chair leaders in a unique position to demonstrate care for their first chairs. While they may not fully understand the weight of the role, second chairs have a greater appreciation than anyone else within the church or ministry. Their tenure and regular interaction allows them to sense almost instantly when something is wrong. And in those moments, second chairs have a unique opportunity to help their first chairs in ways that no one else can.

It may feel strange to offer this kind of care. You may be thinking, *Who am I to ask my boss if everything's okay? Is it really appropriate to go to her office and ask if something is bugging her?* So let me frame this differently. If not you, then who will do it? And if it's an issue that is significantly impacting her leadership, shouldn't you speak up, not only for her sake but also for yours and the organization's?

My former senior pastor announced his retirement plans a month before the 2008 stock market meltdown. In addition to the normal stress of preparing for retirement, he was dealing with enormous upheaval in his financial plans. There were several times in the ensuing months when I was able to go into his office, close the door, and ask, "How are you really doing?" I felt the freedom to do this because of the rich relationship that we had developed over a decade. I felt the obligation to do it because I could see his anxiety and knew that few others could have that conversation with him.

Perhaps you can't do this if you're close to the "autocratic" side of the continuum. But in all probability, there's more opportunity to demonstrate care, and more value from doing so, than you realize.

Pray for your leader. Closely related to demonstrating care is praying regularly for your first chair. It's closely related because as you pray, God will increase your love and compassion for your leader. It will become easier to genuinely care.

If we are to "pray for kings and everyone who is in authority" (1 Tim 2:2), surely our first chair leader is deserving of our prayers. Ask how you can pray for him or her, or share a specific way that you have prayed. As you pray for your first chair, God's Spirit may speak to you in unexpected ways. You may gain new insights on how to practice some of the other steps described in this chapter. You may realize ways that you're blocking the development of the relationship. Praying for your leader can be a powerful catalyst for a stronger relationship.

Be patient. If you're looking for a few easy steps that will move your relationship from one mile to one millimeter within a few months, you don't understand the nature of second chair leadership. As stated earlier, relationships that fit the definition of a partnership take time, generally far more time than expected by the first or second chair leaders. So as you work on the other steps to move along the continuum, do so with patience.

Two Pictures of Partnership

Understanding the definition of a partnership is helpful. So are concrete ideas for advancing along the partnership continuum. But one of the best tests of a partnership comes in unplanned events. Two examples show what can happen in these unscripted moments.

Imagine that you're the associate director (second chair) of a nonprofit ministry. You've worked closely with the executive director (first chair) for four years. You'd say that your relationship fits the definition of a partnership. The two of you are looking forward to tonight's meeting of the board of directors, where they will be asked to approve a major initiative to expand the ministry.

It's a little over an hour before the board meeting and the exec's cell phone rings. It's her husband, and as you hear one end of the conversation, you can tell that something is wrong. When the call ends, she explains that her twelve-year-old son fell awkwardly at soccer practice and may have broken his arm. They're on the way to the emergency room for X-rays and want to know if she can meet them there.

Your first chair has a tough decision to make. She can call the board chair and cancel the meeting, knowing that he will understand. The new initiative is important, but everyone understands that family comes first. Or she can tell her husband that this is a critical board meeting and that she will come to the hospital as soon as possible. She knows that her son is in good hands with the doctors and with his loving dad, and she's sure (sort of) that her husband will understand the importance of this meeting. Or she can ask you to represent her in the meeting so that she can go to the hospital. Which option will she choose?

The third option can only be considered in a partnership. For all the conversations that you may have had about working as partners, this is a moment that puts those ideas to the test. Why would the executive not choose the third option? It could be control or insecurity issues, which are discussed in the next chapter. But apart from this, the most likely reason is that you're not far enough along on the partnership continuum. Something is missing, whether it's a trust issue or a slight strategic misalignment or a competence question. On the other hand, if you're given this kind of authority, it's a clear sign of a partnership at work.

The example above focuses on strategic decision-making, but another scenario can reveal a very different aspect of partnership. You've been the executive pastor for three years, but you've worked closely with your senior pastor for eight years, having served in a key volunteer leadership role before leaving the marketplace to join the staff in this newly created position. While the transition has been harder than you expected, you love working at the church and are confident that you've added tremendous value in your role.

You can see how your relationship with your senior pastor has moved along the continuum, and you would say that you're operating in a true partnership or something that is very close. There have been points on which you've disagreed, as in any close relationship, but you've both handled these well.

Then one day, one of the church's key lay leaders tells the senior pastor that he overheard you voice concerns about a recent decision to change the Sunday morning schedule. This has been a difficult decision, and you did have a different opinion when your senior pastor presented the idea to you. You've worked hard to prevent any differences from becoming public, so you're not sure what this leader may have heard. Perhaps someone asked you about the proposed schedule change, and you had a tone of caution in your voice or described some of the challenges that would need to be addressed.

At this point, what you did (or didn't do) is less important than how your senior pastor will respond to this revelation. Will he believe the lay leader? Or will he think that this doesn't sound like you and give you the benefit of the doubt? Will he come to discuss this with you? If you acknowledge a mistake and apologize, will your apology be truly accepted?

Any time that a second chair appears to have done something that undermines the first chair, it creates a serious strain on the relationship. But in a partnership, where trust levels are high, the first chair should be more likely to doubt the story than to doubt the second chair. And if there is truth to the story, that same trust will allow forgiveness to be extended and experienced much more genuinely and quickly.

A true partnership is a rare but wonderful experience, especially for a second chair leader. If this describes your context, be grateful. It makes it easy to thrive in the second chair. The other springs that quench your thirst for thriving tend to fall into place or become less important when you're treated as a partner. Don't take the relationship for granted.

For the rest of you, don't be discouraged that you're not experiencing a true partnership. Realize that it's much easier to say the words than to actually create one. Know that you're not alone. And know that in the end, you don't control your movement up the continuum. That is ultimately a decision that is controlled by your first chair. The only thing you can do is to take the steps that will help your first chair see you as a potential partner.

Sometimes they will. But when they don't, there are nine other springs for thriving that can still be part of your journey.

The end of each chapter includes several questions to help you engage further with the material and take the next steps toward thriving. These are divided into two sections: one for your personal reflection and one for you to discuss with your first chair leader. Before the initial discussion, first chair leaders may want to read appendix B, "A First Chair's Guide to Thriving," which will give them an overview of the book.

Personal Reflection

- Do you desire a partnership with your first chair as defined in this chapter?
- In what ways is your relationship a partnership? In what ways does it fall short?
- Where are you on the continuum between one mile and one millimeter?
- What steps do you personally need to take to move along the partnership continuum?

Discuss with Your First Chair

- Review the definition of partnership. Do you agree with this? What does this mean to each of you?
- What are the benefits of having a true partnership?
- Do you have a high level of trust as described in this chapter? If not, why not? What needs to happen to build trust?
- Is the vision clear for your church or ministry? If not, what needs to be clarified?
- First chairs: Discuss any concerns about the second chair (performance, attitude, etc.) that are barriers to a partnership.
- Agree on any steps that you will both commit to so that you can move toward a partnership.

Chapter 2

Live with (and Lift) the "Lid"

Thriving second chairs seek to be catalysts for their first chair's growth while remaining patient with the weaknesses.

"What do you wish you had written differently?" is one of the most common questions for an author. For me, the answer has been clear and consistent for ten years. I wish that we had helped second chair leaders deal with a first chair leader's weaknesses. In some cases, these aren't just weaknesses—they can be described as dysfunctions.

This issue is wrapped up in the *subordinate*-leader paradox of second chair leadership.[1] None of us readily embrace the word *subordination.* We prefer words like *partner* or *colleague* or *teammate.* But the reality is that the first chair leader is the boss, and second chair leaders will never be successful if they don't understand that they are in a subordinate role.

Under ideal circumstances, the supervisor-subordinate relationship is characterized by positive, healthy collaboration in which the first chair rarely, if ever, plays the "boss card." Rather, the two share a common vision and are able to stay on the same page. Within that broad direction, second chairs do their jobs with a high level of autonomy and little "interference" from the first chair. When issues arise, they are dealt with in direct and healthy ways.

This sounds great. But like any "ideal," it is rarely achieved. And even when your relationship does come close to the ideal, you are still in a subordinate

1. The three paradoxes from *Leading from the Second Chair* are summarized in appendix A of this book.

role. That is when your ability to understand and embrace the subordinate-leader paradox will be tested.

One of John Maxwell's *21 Irrefutable Laws of Leadership* is the "Law of the Lid," in which he states that a person's leadership ability determines their effectiveness.[2] Maxwell's message is for self-aware and motivated leaders who want to improve by lifting their own "lids." But it's different if you're the one seeing the gaps in your boss's skill set. That lid affects you and your church or ministry. If the first chair's lid is heavy enough, does that mean that thriving in the second chair is impossible?

Recognizing the Lids

What are these lids? If you have ever said, "I just wish that my first chair . . . ," you have pointed to a potential leadership lid. Perhaps you finished the sentence with a phrase like "trusted me more" or "had a clearer vision" or "didn't change directions so frequently" or "wouldn't run from conflict." Whatever phrase you would insert in this blank indicates an area where your first chair falls short of your ideal. The gap between this ideal and your first chair's actual ability may be one of his or her leadership lids.

For example, consider the first phrase, "trusted me more." Assume that your second chair role includes oversight of much of the staff in your church or ministry. From your perspective, the broad strategy is set by the leadership team, the budget is determined by the finance team, and the organization structure is established by the personnel team. You and the first chair participate on each of these teams.

These three elements (strategy, budget, and organization structure) give you the parameters that you need to oversee the staff. You expect to be able to make the day-to-day decisions such as shifting duties based on priorities and abilities, recruiting and selecting people to fill positions, coaching or correcting staff to achieve goals, and even firing people who have consistently failed to meet expectations. You know that major decisions—hiring or firing a key position—require discussion with the first chair. But you get frustrated when he sticks his hand in the smaller, routine decisions. You ask the youth intern to edit a video because the communications person is swamped, and then the pastor asks why. You tell the development director that her lack of organization is hurting her performance,

2. John C. Maxwell, *The 21 Irrefutable Laws of Leadership: Follow Them and People Will Follow You* (Nashville: Thomas Nelson, 1998), chapter 1.

and your boss questions you for being so negative. It is in moments like these that you say, "I wish that my first chair trusted me more."

Before you slap the "untrusting" label on your first chair, you would do well to keep three principles in mind:

- The real issue may be deeper or different than what you initially see. You perceive a lack of trust, but the underlying issue may be the first chair's need for control. This may be evidenced in various kinds of micromanagement that go far beyond personnel decisions and that affect others on the staff.
- Your frustration with one particular incident doesn't necessarily make it a lid. You may have just caught your first chair on a bad day or pushed a hot button. Don't rush to judgment if you don't see a broader pattern.
- There are often two sides to the coin of perceived leadership deficiencies. You may see the first chair as not extending enough trust and not giving you enough autonomy. But trust and autonomy can go too far. The opposite side of that coin is a "free agent" culture where there are few boundaries and every staff member chooses what he or she will work on.

In describing these basic principles, I am not suggesting that every difficult situation can be easily explained away. Some first chair behavior is a lid, and at times it can even be dysfunctional, as we'll explore later in this chapter. But before trying to determine if the object in our first chair's eye is a speck or something bigger, we need to examine the plank in our own eye (Matt 7:3-5).

Start with Yourself

When a married couple is dealing with relational tension, one of the fundamental premises is that each person needs to work on his and her own issues rather than trying to "fix" the other. This concept does not deny the reality of the other spouse's contribution to the problem. It does not make any assumption about who is more at fault. It simply recognizes that the most productive path to healing begins with you.

In the same way, second chair leaders who are frustrated with their first chair's shortcomings should begin with self-examination. You may think that the problem rests 100 percent on your first chair's shoulders, but this is rarely the case. It's natural to jump to questions such as "How can I show him the damage that he is causing?" or "What can I do to get her to change?" The starting point, however, should be asking three questions of yourself:

- How might I be contributing to the problem?
- Why am I so sensitive to this aspect of my first chair's behavior?
- What do I need to learn from this situation?

Andrew, who was the contemporary worship leader at his church, was frustrated at his first chair's lack of collaboration. It seemed that the senior pastor made all the decisions, including decisions about worship that directly affected Andrew. He attributed this to the first chair being an "old school" pastor with a top-down leadership style. At one time, Andrew had been included in more of the meetings where those decisions were made. What he failed to realize is that he tended to over-talk the smallest details and rarely asked for input from others. In frustration, his senior pastor had changed the decision-making process to exclude Andrew. While this may not have been the best approach—the senior pastor should have coached Andrew—the reality is that Andrew was part of the problem.

Even if you are not part of the problem, you may be particularly sensitive to one of your first chair's tendencies. You describe a behavior as a lid that clearly needs to be addressed. Someone else experiences the same behavior as normal. When your first chair asks for a detailed review of your work on a project, you label it as a "lack of trust," but one of your colleagues calls it "normal management."

Personality, training, and past experiences are all part of the equation that can cause second chairs to struggle with specific behavior by a first chair. One of my "hot buttons" is frequent changes in direction. By personality, I am highly structured. My education in engineering and business reinforce this tendency. In my professional experience, my orderliness and ability to plan ahead have led to successful outcomes. I have also seen organizations flounder because of constantly changing strategies. Given all of these personal factors, it is no wonder that I am particularly sensitive to this behavior.

Thriving second chair leaders engage in personal reflection when they feel a rising frustration with their first chair. If someone else has the same experience but is not frustrated, this may indicate that the real issue is the second chair's sensitivity rather than the first chair's leadership lid.

The third question is just as important: What do you need to learn? Some of this learning relates to the first two questions, but it is possible that God has other lessons to teach you. Our greatest growth often comes in challenging times. It's a pleasure to be mentored by a good boss, but we can also learn from those who are less than stellar. When your first chair fails to recognize your contributions, it stings. It is also an opportunity for you to make a deep mental commitment to act differently and be more appreciative of others.

Many years ago, I worked for someone with terrible time management skills. This led to many late nights for me because his input on projects always came at the last minute. I also observed a number of occasions when he made last-minute calls to his wife to tell her that he would miss dinner or other family commitments. In those moments, I recognized that I also had a tendency to let work come before family, and I made a decision to live differently.

The value in asking these three questions is incalculable. They will help you become a better leader and a better person. They will enable you to gain a different perspective on your first chair's leadership. In some cases, you will realize that there is nothing you need to address. And in the cases where there truly is a problem, you will have already shown a willingness to change yourself and will be much better positioned to raise the concern with your first chair.

The Biggest Lid

No one is a perfect leader—not you, and not your first chair. But some behaviors and traits go beyond the simple label of "imperfection." These are characteristics that significantly hinder a leader's effectiveness. Left unaddressed, they can derail the relationship between first and second chairs and cause the church or ministry to fall far short of its potential. While there are a variety of common lids, one stands out and is often the root of others.

Over a cup of coffee, a friend described a list of frustrations with his senior pastor. I commented that this senior pastor appeared to be quite insecure in his leadership. My friend responded, "All senior pastors are insecure." At first, his statement took me aback, but I think it contains a great deal of truth. Even if it overstates the case to say that insecurity is a characteristic of every first chair in ministry, it is a widespread problem that merits further examination.

The reality is that church and ministry leaders have many reasons to be insecure:

- The context in which they are doing ministry continues to change at an accelerating pace. Future results can't be found in the past or present. Success is not predictable nor is it guaranteed.
- Most feel ill-equipped in the training that they have received. Their education included little, if any, leadership development and they may have been mentored by people whose wisdom comes from a different era.
- They need to continually lead change in organizations that consistently resist it. Churches and ministries are notorious for the many obstacles that they put in the path of the very efforts that could lead to renewed vitality.
- The base of constituents is fragmented in a church or a ministry. This makes it harder to read the mood of the organization, more challenging to build a coalition, and ultimately more difficult to lead.
- Job security is nonexistent. Every ministry leader knows horror stories of a colleague who lost a job with no warning and minimal severance pay. In appointive systems, it may look different, but sudden changes are still a possibility. Combined with the previous reasons, many leaders feel that a bullet with their name on it is always headed their way.
- Ministry leadership carries an enormous weight of responsibility. The incredible opportunity to partner with God in life transformation comes with the possibility of "failing." Every ministry leader wants to hear, "Well done, good and faithful servant" at the finish line. Many worry that they will somehow fall short of this commendation.

Randy had been very confident as a second chair leader. It was reflected in his decisions and in his demeanor. But everything changed when he stepped into the first chair role. He was slower to make decisions and often chose the path of least resistance. At one point, he told his staff, "I was much more certain of what to do when I sat in the second chair than I am today." The insecurities in his leadership in those early years as a first chair reflected many of the factors listed above.

Insecurity affects how the first chair leader relates to others. Insecure first chairs often choose close advisors and confidants that readily agree with them. They will regularly look for affirmation and will push away people who are critical. In many cases, they will display a confident public image to hide the uncertainty they feel.

It may be true that "all first chair leaders" are somewhat insecure. This insecurity rises to the level of being dysfunctional when they are incapable of making important decisions. They may waffle back and forth depending on who they talked to most recently. They may procrastinate, putting the decision off as long as possible (and then a little longer). They may become completely paralyzed.

Another manifestation of insecurity is resentment toward a competent second chair. The very best matches of first and second chair leaders occur when their gifts are complementary. Of course, having complementary gifts implies that the second chair excels in some areas where the first chair is weak. Some first chairs can't stand the idea of admitting a weakness or of hearing how their second chair is better in some dimension of leadership. In these cases, they may try to choose second chairs that won't outshine them or they may limit the second chair's role.

Other Common Lids

As you can see, and may have experienced, insecurity can be a critical and crippling issue for first chair leaders and the second chairs who serve with them. There is not a magic wand that will transform someone into a secure leader, but there are steps that a second chair can take toward thriving in these situations. We'll look at those later in this chapter, after we consider other common lids.

Lack of Vision

It's been almost twenty years, but I still remember the question. I was teaching a conference on leading congregational change when a second chair leader, in this case a layperson, raised his hand and said: "Our pastor doesn't seem to have a vision. Can we discern the vision without him?"

Unfortunately, that isn't the only time that I've been asked this question. Lack of vision is a common leadership lid. In some cases, the root issue is insecurity.

The first chair may have a clear idea of where the church or ministry needs to go, but she is reluctant to state this publicly for fear of criticism, rejection, or worse.

In other cases, what some followers perceive to be a lack of vision may be better described as an unclear vision. This is a valid concern that it is often voiced by detail-oriented second chairs. An effective vision is much more than a catchy phrase that captures the imagination of the people. It ultimately needs to be accompanied by answers to questions such as "What does this mean?" and "What do we need to do?" These questions are not typically answered in a "vision statement." They are answered in the plans developed out of the vision. Left unanswered, this lack of clarity may lead some to feel that vision is lacking.

Yet another variation relates to timing. Second chairs who are action oriented and impatient by nature may express this frustration. There is a big difference between a lack of vision and not yet sensing a clear direction from God.

The regional denominational body had endured months of chaos after the abrupt departure of its previous leader. When Charlotte stepped into the first chair role, she immediately saw the need to address staff morale and service-quality issues, but she also felt the pressure to develop a new vision. Several important strategic decisions were looming, including expanding their church planting initiative, restructuring the staff, and eliminating ineffective programs. Six months into her tenure, Charlotte was still cleaning up messes. She knew that this would take several more months and wasn't ready to launch any new initiatives or make other major changes. What some perceived as a complete lack of vision was really more an issue of timing.

True lack of vision is a challenge for some first chair leaders. Discerning a bold and compelling vision is simply not their gift. No matter how much they are encouraged or prodded to develop this kind of picture of the future, they are unable to do so. This may limit how far the church or ministry can go, but it may also be an opportunity for a second chair to play a pivotal role in partnership with the first chair.

Too Much Vision

I encounter far more questions about "too much vision" than I do about a lack of vision. This leadership issue is expressed in two related, but distinct, variations.

The vision may be so big and bold that a second chair's immediate reaction is, "There is no way that we can accomplish that." Sometimes the vision truly is too big. The first chair may have produced a grand statement that has little basis in reality. This may be his own inclination, or he may have felt pressure from key constituents or peers to "dream big." Frequently, he will not understand all the steps that are needed to implement the vision. If you press him for details, he will answer vaguely, "We'll figure it out." Or he will look at you and say, "Working out the details is your job."

The problem with slapping the "deficiency" label on this leadership tendency is that an audacious vision might be impossible, but it might also be exactly right. Twenty years ago, a small number of pastors had visions that God might want to expand their congregations through the use of satellite campuses. At the time, the number of details to work out seemed almost insurmountable, and the number of critics of this idea was even greater. Today, multisite congregations are widespread and widely accepted.

A more problematic version of too much vision is "vision du jour," the tendency of some first chair leaders to change directions and priorities on a regular basis. In this case, it's more accurate to say that they have too many visions. This can create organizational whiplash, which frustrates people and wastes resources. Of course, no first chair leader intends to have this kind of negative impact. Some are too easily influenced by outside factors, so they follow the latest fad or success story. Others are impatient and give up before a new initiative has had a chance to succeed. Still others are easily bored and are always looking for the next shiny, new thing.

When dealing with this leadership weakness, a second chair will end up holding her breath every time the first chair gets a twinkle in his eye and says, "I have an idea!" She may develop an involuntary "no" reflex and become the person who always rains on the first chair's parade. This will eventually create unhealthy relational stress or cause the second chair's voice to be marginalized.

Too Spontaneous

The first chair leader of your church or ministry needs to be someone who prayerfully seeks God's direction and makes decisions in light of this. Of course, that means that God may interrupt or redirect plans at times. While this may come across as spontaneity, it can actually be healthy Spirit-guided leadership. Somewhere along the spectrum, however, a line can be crossed where last-minute changes become an ingrained habit and "spiritual guidance" becomes an excuse for poor planning.

Over the years that Jack had been the senior pastor, the church had grown much larger and had added several worship services. The worship team was full of talented people who had proven their ability to design powerful services. There was only one problem—Jack usually decided the title and focus of his sermon just a few days in advance. He would routinely commit to getting further ahead, but when he delivered a last-minute idea, he explained that he was waiting on God to speak to him. Over time, the team grew increasingly cynical about the source of Jack's inspiration.

Just like the first chair with too much vision, a leader's abundance of spontaneity can be exhausting to the church or ministry. It can lead to poor use of resources and tension between the leader and the staff. And it can put the second chair in the middle of a difficult situation.

Too Demanding

A first chair leader's success is always by God's grace, but it usually comes through hard work as well. These leaders often demand much of themselves, and they have the same high standards for others. High expectations are good—up to a point. But some first chairs go well beyond this point and become excessively demanding of second chairs and the rest of the staff. In the worst cases, their tyrant-like behavior may even be described as abusive.

When high expectations become dysfunctional demands, this can have a widespread impact on a church or ministry. Turnover becomes common as individuals who were thrilled to have an opportunity to work for a prominent ministry become disenchanted once they see what it's really like on the inside. Those who stay become burned out and lose effectiveness as their frustration spills over into the quality of their work.

A different variation of "demanding" is with leaders who are highly autocratic. They have strong opinions on what should be done and leave little room for other ideas. Whether they speak softly or loudly, they know what they want and they make sure that staff members know as well.

In either of these environments, other leaders often learn to stay quiet, in one case to avoid harsh rebukes and in the other because it does no good to speak. Unfortunately, this silence translates into missed opportunities. Important problems are left unaddressed and collaboration becomes the exception rather than the norm.

Not Thriving

This book focuses on helping second chair leaders thrive, but doing so becomes difficult if the first chair isn't thriving. Second chairs, and the churches or ministries they serve, depend on energetic, Spirit-filled leadership from the person in the first chair. It's hard to move the organization forward if the person in the lead role doesn't demonstrate vitality and a passion for the mission.

Any number of factors can cause a senior pastor or executive director to lose enthusiasm. They may encounter serious resistance from within the church or ministry. This is particularly troubling when it comes in the form of personal attacks or when the resistors are key leaders or friends. Some first chairs are plagued by uncertainty about whether they are steering the organization in the right direction. If the results are poor, or even just less than expected, they often feel a sense of personal responsibility that can be crippling. In some cases, a lack of passion is really a growing sense that God may be leading the first chair to a new assignment.

Even in good times, first chairs can experience a level of fatigue that prevents thriving. When a leader feels like a hamster on the never-ending wheel, hope will disappear. Another good news–bad news scenario occurs when a leader completes a major objective, and then lacks a new challenge. The bottom line is that a second chair's ability to thrive is inevitably intertwined with that of their first chair.

People Pleaser

A lid that affects many ministry leaders is the desire to maintain happiness and peace within the organization at all times. Don't get me wrong—I'm not suggesting that leaders should be heartless or that they shouldn't care about the people they lead. That's a different kind of dysfunction, but it's one that is much less common in ministry settings. It's not a deficiency to consider people's feelings and how they might react before making leadership decisions. It is a problem, however, if those concerns immobilize a leader.

Rob, the senior pastor of a large church, had spent the last several weeks working on a new organization chart for the staff. After receiving input on the various options, he asked Mark to step into the role of executive pastor. Rob explained that this would mean overseeing all of the staff. Rob met with three other key staff members before announcing the plan to the entire team. By the end of those meetings, each of the three had been repositioned to report directly to Rob instead of Mark. Lindsey, who had always reported to Rob, didn't think that it was fair to be "demoted" after years of faithful service. Steve reminded Rob of tension that had existed between him and Mark, and hinted that he would quit if this new structure was implemented. The worship leader, Shannon, wondered if the worship services would lose some of their creativity with "Mark in the middle."

While their arguments had merit, the driving factor in Rob's reversal was a desire to keep the peace and to be "liked" by these three. If a first chair is incapable of making a decision, or always chooses the safest and least controversial path, it's a sign that people pleasing may have become a lid.

Not a Leader

A final perceived deficiency is the first chair who is "not a leader." I do not find this to be a helpful or meaningful description. What does it mean when someone is labeled in this way? Sometimes "not a leader" is applied to a person based on the organization's results. If the church or ministry is declining, it is fair to question the leader's effectiveness. It is also appropriate to look at other factors.

The first chair may truly lack the gift of leadership, but "not a leader" often refers to one of the previously described lids. In particular, insecurity, lack of vision, or a strong desire to please people all give the appearance of weak leadership. A more precise diagnosis is needed before any constructive steps can be taken.

At times, the first chair is a leader, but not the kind of leader that's expected. A church that wants an extroverted pastor may say that the introvert in the senior role is "not a leader," regardless of qualifications or results. A ministry's board may want someone who will take charge, so the consensus-oriented executive director is tagged with the nonleader designation. Sometimes it's a matter of individual, not organizational, expectations. If you define a "good leader" as someone who is highly relational, does that mean they're not a leader if they are more businesslike and task-oriented?

The old adage is true that "you can't please all the people all the time." Before deciding that your first chair is "not a leader," examine the reason for your conclusion and move toward an assessment that will help lift the lid.

Lifting the Lid

Perhaps one of the leadership lids in the previous section resonated with you. Perhaps more than one. After all, they're not mutually exclusive. In fact, some of them tend to go together. Insecurity exacerbates a desire to please others. Some pastors who have too much vision become very demanding because of their urgency to achieve the vision. At the same time, others who lack vision can also become overbearing in hopes that their staff will make something happen. The same lack of vision will cause yet others to be insecure at the fact that they're being asked for a vision.

Regardless of how these interact, second chair leaders need to decide whether they can play a role in lifting the first chair's leadership lid, and if so, how. Let's assume that you're already actively working on Step Zero—conducting a self-examination and addressing the ways that you may be contributing to the problem. Let's also assume that you've been able to step back to calmly evaluate the situation, and you're confident that the behavior in question truly is a deficiency and not just minor annoyance.

If you find yourself in this position, it's time to act by starting the conversation with your first chair. Just that phrase—"time to act"—may trigger a burst of anxiety for you. Isn't it risky to point out a leadership weakness to your first chair? There's no way to make the conversation risk-free, but not acting also has a cost. How does this lid impact you and the organization? What are the missed opportunities that are caused by the leadership lid?

You may wonder why you should be the one to act. Isn't that a job for the governance body? In many ways it is, except that second chairs often have a clearer perspective and closer relationship that enables them to have this difficult conversation.

So what does it mean to act? If you want to help your first chair lift a leadership lid, you need to discern, build trust, tiptoe first, demonstrate the impact, offer solutions, and affirm.

Discern. You've already begun to practice discernment in deciding whether the issue truly represents a leadership lid, but there's more discerning to be done. To the best of your ability, try to understand the real reason for this behavior.

I'm not asking you to play amateur psychologist and to develop a clinical diagnosis. But you can pay attention to the formative stories from your first chair's life, to the current context, and to the things that trigger the undesirable behavior. What seems to prompt fear or stress? What painful stories has he or she shared from the past? As you pay attention, you will gain new, valuable insights.

Discerning also means trying to determine if change is possible and in what time frame. My friend Judy West, who stands five feet and one-half inch high, refers to the "I can't grow taller" scenario. She says, "You can tell me to grow taller as many times as you want. You can put me in heels for a few hours. You can talk to others. But I cannot grow taller." If you discern that the change you'd like to see is asking your first chair to "grow taller," then recognize the futility of this pursuit.

Even if the change is possible, it may take time. A new first chair might become more secure with experience, but it won't happen overnight. An operationally oriented leader who is not a visionary may not ever have a bold, audacious dream for the ministry's future but might be able to move beyond short-term, tactical thinking. Thoughtful and prayerful discernment should help you decide what's at the heart of the deficiency and whether to address it.

Build trust. As highlighted in the previous chapter, trust is the key ingredient for effective relationships between first and second chair leaders. Nowhere is this more apparent than when you're trying to address a leadership weakness. You may have the best of intentions, but without a strong foundation of trust, your words can easily be interpreted as insubordination.

Imagine that you're starting a difficult conversation with your senior pastor about the chaos that is caused by his vision du jour. You know this won't be an easy conversation, but you're convinced that it's appropriate. You start the conversation by saying, "You know that I genuinely care about you and our church, so please know that what I'm about to say is with the best of intentions." If your pastor doesn't trust you at a deep level, the conversation may be derailed before you even start. He doesn't know (or at least doesn't trust) that you genuinely care. The opening only puts him on the defensive. If trust is high, he still may get defensive as you deliver your message, but he will be less likely to question your good intentions.

Think of trust as a bridge. When trust is low, it's like a rickety suspension bridge that won't carry the weight of a difficult, critical message. When trust is high, it's like a sturdy highway bridge that can carry enormous weight. Hard conversations about leadership lids are weighty, and they can't be addressed without trust.

Tiptoe first. In almost any case where you decide to move forward, it's best to tiptoe. The deficiency that you're addressing isn't something that's trivial or superficial. Even if a high level of trust exists between you and the first chair, you can't run across the bridge. The best way to approach someone about a leadership lid, especially if they are insecure, is by taking one small step at a time.

In practice, this means you will probably have multiple conversations about the concern. If you expect to conquer a major issue in one sitting, you're sure to experience disappointment or worse. A first step may be to point out one specific instance of the problematic behavior. Or you may ask some gentle questions to see if the first chair is aware of her tendencies. The goal of tiptoeing is to open the door for a conversation, not to solve the problem instantly.

Demonstrate the impact. Change is never easy, whether at an organizational or personal level. Once you get beyond the first steps, you will be asking your first chair to change. So if you want to have a chance at convincing him to lift his leadership lid, you'll need to demonstrate the impact that it has on the organization. Your explanation will need to offer concrete examples and show that the concern is a pattern, not an isolated incident. If the alleged problem is only a one-time or infrequent occurrence or if it's too abstract, it will be easy for your first chair to shrug it off.

The ultra-spontaneous pastor needs to see that staff members are frustrated by the constant changes in direction and that they can't produce high-quality work if they get last-minute instructions. The highly visionary pastor needs to understand the fatigue of a staff that's trying to keep up or the trail of incomplete projects that have been created by shifting to a new vision.

If your appeal sounds like whining, once again it will be easy for your first chair to shrug it off. There may be times when you're the only one who is significantly impacted by a first chair's negative behavior. If so, think twice before bringing it to her attention. She has plenty of other concerns, and she may simply tell you to get over it, especially if it sounds as though you're just complaining.

The challenge of demonstrating the impact is that you're not tiptoeing any longer. To raise a first chair's awareness enough to move toward change, they must see the real consequences. Any way you cut it, it's a difficult conversation with an unpredictable outcome.

Offer solutions. The best conversations about leadership lids include ideas for how the lid can be lifted. Even though this will ultimately be the responsibility of the first chair, second chairs can make valuable contributions. They have a fresh, outside perspective on the need. They also have had time to think about the concern and how it might be resolved.

A pastor who is prone to pleasing people may have a tendency to say "yes" to every idea that is proposed. You may consider making it harder for people to get an appointment to pitch a new idea, or attending these meetings with him to counterbalance his tendency. You might create a vetting process and then invite him to say, "That's a great idea, and now I'd like you to take this next step..."

Offering possible solutions is a pragmatic part of the process for helping your first chair lift a leadership lid. It also demonstrates that you're not trying to criticize but that you genuinely care. This is reinforced in the final element—affirming your first chair.

Affirm. Affirmation is one of the most frequently overlooked tools when second chair leaders are initiating difficult conversations with their first chairs. Perhaps that's because it feels strange to affirm the boss. Or maybe it's because the first chair seems confident and you think that she gets plenty of kudos. It may be that you've wrestled with the lid for so long that you're not in an affirming mood.

Just know this. Most first chairs need far more encouragement than you might guess. They may not ask for it and may not give any indication of their need, but in most cases the desire exists at a deep level. When that difficult conversation starts, it's easy for them to start to hear disloyalty or to think that a valued second chair may be on the brink of leaving. If you want to preserve your relationship and improve your chances of lifting the lid, be sure to include affirmation.

When the Lid Can't Be Lifted

Of all the springs that lead to thriving, this has been the most difficult to write about. The overall tone of this chapter has balanced the reality of a first chair's weaknesses with the hope that these lids can be lifted. But some of you are dealing with lids that seem to be stuck in place. You refer to this as dysfunction, not deficiency. You don't see growth areas but rather insurmountable problems that are crippling the church or ministry. I know this because I've heard too many stories over the years from second chair leaders who feel that a heavy lid makes it impossible to thrive.

I've struggled to write this chapter because there are no easy answers or quick fixes if you find yourself in this situation. The last thing I want to do is suggest that it's not really that bad. Perhaps the earlier pages have given you a fresh and more hopeful perspective, but if you're still convinced that the lid can't be lifted, then what should you do? In this case, two of the later springs for thriving become indispensable. It is essential that you stay anchored spiritually (chapter 8) and not allow yourself to be isolated (chapter 9).

In addition, it is possible to find joy in the ministry to which God has called you, even in the midst of a difficult season. It may come in your relationships with other staff members or in certain activities that feed your soul or in places where God is at work despite the leadership limitations. When the lid feels heaviest, pour your time and energy into those places, and let Paul's instructions to rejoice always and think on good things (Phil 4:4, 8) wash over you.

This is also a time to pray for God's guidance. All second chair leaders should hold loosely to the roles they are in, whether they're soaring or struggling. But in times of struggle, especially when days turn into weeks or months, it's appropriate to ask God if your current season is coming to a close. Perhaps God has a place that will better use your gifts, or you're simply no longer the "right" second chair for your church or ministry. Don't let your worries about "what will happen if I leave?" keep you in a place if God is calling you to go. And don't let your frustrations cause you to leave before God is ready for you to do so.

The problem with using the "lid" analogy is that it seems so simple. But whether you need to live with a lid or work ever so slowly to lift it, you know that doing so is anything but simple. Thriving is not about removing the lid—it's being lovingly patient with a fellow leader's weaknesses, being confident that you're where God has called you to be, and celebrating moments of progress when the lid begins to lift.

Personal Reflection

- Review the three questions on page 26. What do you need to learn from these?
- Did you identify a specific leadership lid that concerns you? Is it one that needs to be lifted?
- Ask a trusted friend to give you feedback on ways that you may be incorrectly interpreting some aspect of your first chair's behavior as a leadership "lid."
- Review the steps in the section on "lifting the lid." What will you say in the conversation with your first chair?

Discuss with Your First Chair

- Are both of you willing to have this discussion? Is your relationship healthy enough to talk about "lids"?
- Second chairs: Ask your first chair how he or she prefers for you to voice concerns or frustrations about his or her leadership, now and in the future.
- If the first chair is willing, discuss the fears or insecurities that are affecting his or her leadership. What are the underlying causes of this insecurity?
- Discuss the specific leadership concern. If appropriate, develop a plan to address this concern.

Chapter 3

Clarify Your Role

Second chair leaders know that there will always be ambiguity in their roles, so they thrive by living in the balance between pursuing clarity and demonstrating flexibility.

"And all other duties as may be assigned." This is commonly the last line in a job description, but the practical reality for many second chair leaders is that it is their first responsibility. This simple truth can be frustrating and confusing.

It's confusing when you're not sure what your priorities should be or when you can't plan your day. It's frustrating if you feel as though your performance will be evaluated based on an arbitrary set of expectations or if you feel that your time or talents are being wasted. You may wonder why it's so difficult to develop a job description or if you're the only one who has these struggles.

You're not. When I'm working with a group of second chair leaders, I often ask them to think about their job description (written or verbal). Then I ask them to reflect on how well their actual jobs match this description. This usually results in a moment of laughter as well as a new awareness that they're not alone in their lack of role clarity.

The challenges of second chair role clarity tend to fall into one of five categories:

- Responsibilities and expectations for the job are not well defined at all.

- Responsibilities were well defined at one time, but the current reality is quite different.
- A significant gap exists between responsibilities and authority.
- The second chair leader has gifts and abilities that aren't being used.
- A transition has occurred—either in the first chair or within the executive team.

Which of these resonates with you? It's possible that more than one of these issues is impacting your ability to thrive. Remember that it's not necessary to eliminate all ambiguity in order to thrive. But it is important to understand the sources of tension and address them as much as possible.

When the Role Is Not Well Defined

In those same workshops where I ask second chair leaders about their roles, someone inevitably tells me that they've never had anything that would pass for a written or verbal job description. Perhaps there was a brief conversation about the position or a few bullet points written on a napkin over lunch one day, but it was never formalized. This is most common when someone is promoted into a second chair role from within the church or ministry, or when a church member is brought onto the staff in a newly created second chair position.

In these cases, "all other duties as may be assigned" isn't just the primary responsibility for the job. It becomes the only responsibility because of the lack of other defined duties.

Vagueness is the hallmark of this challenge. For example, the senior pastor may have said, "I need you to help me manage the staff." What does that mean? Do staff members report to the first chair or the second chair? What "help" is needed? Which "staff" are you helping to manage? Or a first chair may have stated that your primary job is to "implement the vision." Is the vision clear? Are you responsible for interpreting the vision at the next level of detail? How much freedom do you have to implement?

From your perspective, it seems obvious that some sort of job description is appropriate and helpful. But what about from your first chair's perspective? Here are three reasons your first chair may not have defined your job well:

- The first chair is the classic visionary. He simply isn't a detail person and doesn't think in these terms. In fact, he would find it difficult to write his own job description.

- A related but slightly different version is the first chair who knows she needs help but doesn't even know what kind of help is possible. This scenario occurs most often when someone feels overloaded by first chair responsibilities. She knows that she has become a bottleneck that keeps the church or ministry from moving forward, but she's not sure what to take off her plate. In most of these cases, the first chair has never worked with a true second chair.

- A more problematic situation is when the board pushes the first chair to hire a second chair. Because it wasn't the first chair's idea, he isn't sure what the role should be, is often resentful of the second chair, and will be reluctant to release much authority.

Even though these three scenarios are quite different, the common denominator is that it is pointless to demand a real job description from your first chair. Demanding will only create tension, not a meaningful job description. Does that mean that you're doomed to live in ambiguity? No, because there is another option.

If you're frustrated that your role is not well defined, you can take the initiative to create clarity. While it may seem odd or even arrogant, second chair leaders in these situations often need to draft (or revise) their own job descriptions.

The key in doing this is the second chair's attitude and intentions. Taking initiative in this way must not be seen as an attempt to usurp authority or undermine the first chair. Effective second chair leaders will ask for permission to create a *draft* job description. They will explain that their purpose is to start a conversation that will bring clarity to their role and fruitfulness to the church or ministry. Conversation is the key. The draft document starts a discussion between the first and second chair that clarifies their roles and how they relate to each other. In most cases, multiple discussions are needed to bring about this clarity.

So if you have permission and know that you need to create a job description, where should you start? Ask yourself the following questions:

- What would most help to advance the mission of our church or ministry? What areas are falling short of their potential? "Areas" could be specific departments, major initiatives, or organization-wide systems. (This question is explored further in chapters 4 and 6.)

- What are my first chair's biggest needs? Where is she overwhelmed? Where does he have leadership gaps that need to be supplemented?

- What am I most passionate about? In what ways will my gifts allow me to make the greatest contribution?

- How should my role be defined so that it moves toward a partnership (chapter 1) and clearly demonstrates my support for the first chair?

When a second chair's job has never been well defined, this process can begin a conversation that brings much-needed clarity to the role. But a job description is only a starting point. It will never fully capture the nuances and the ever-changing dynamics of the second chair.

When the Role Definition Is Outdated

Travis wasn't in a second chair role when he was hired. He reported to the mission agency's associate director (second chair) and was responsible for the recruitment program, which was a central element in their strategy. On his second day on the job, a peer who led another major program resigned, and Travis was asked to add this to his responsibilities. Within a year, Travis had been asked to oversee two other programs, had a total of four people reporting to him, and was a member of the senior leadership team. Even though he still reported to the associate director, he worked closely with the executive director (first chair) on several projects, and he was helping to shape the agency's strategy. Travis was becoming a second chair leader.

During one of the senior leadership team's weekly meetings, the executive and associate directors both expressed concern about the agency's lack of new missionaries. Recruiting had remained one of Travis's direct responsibilities, but it had received much less of his attention as the other duties were added. He was caught off guard by the criticism—after all, it hardly seemed fair that he was being held accountable for the goals of the original full-time job when he now had less than ten hours a week that he could devote to it.

Travis was caught in one of the classic role-clarity issues for second chair leaders—a gap between an outdated set of responsibilities and a new reality. In his case, the expectations for recruitment had never changed from the day when Travis was hired, even though his job had expanded significantly.

The second chair leaders that I know are high-capacity individuals who have a deep desire for their church or ministry to be successful and a drive to accomplish this. Given their zeal and energy, it's no surprise that being bored or underutilized is something they dread. They want to add value wherever possible, so they willingly jump in to help when they see a need. On top of this is the reality that "all other duties" seems to give first chair leaders carte blanche to redefine the job at any time and in any way. These two realities often lead to expanded roles and overloaded second chairs.

So what should you do if you're experiencing this kind of role confusion? Let me start with two responses that are not helpful. If "all other duties" is a reality, then it's ineffective (and perhaps inappropriate) to respond, "That's not my job." Anything can be your job. In some ways, everything is your job. Similarly, it's not productive to say, "That's not what I signed up for." While that may be true in a narrow sense, if you signed up to be a second chair leader, then you signed up to help the first chair and the organization succeed.

What you can do is talk to your first chair. The starting point for your conversation is to point out how much the role has changed and where you feel squeezed. Your first chair may not be aware of this reality. Whenever possible, propose a solution. Your first chair doesn't want to have another problem dumped in his lap. You will find a much more sympathetic audience if you offer viable ways to resolve the issue. (See the section titled "Saying No" in chapter 10 for some related thoughts.)

Second chair leaders who thrive are flexible and are pruners. Your church or ministry will continue to change, and you need to be prepared to change with it. Rigidly clinging to old expectations is not a viable approach. New assignments will be added to your plate on a regular basis. So don't resist or resent new tasks. Instead, make a regular habit of reviewing and pruning—find ways to take things off your plate to create breathing room for fresh challenges.

When Responsibility Exceeds Authority

The gap between expectations and reality can take many forms. One of the most frustrating cases occurs when a second chair is expected to achieve certain results but lacks the authority that should accompany this responsibility.

Sherry had been thrilled at the opportunity to leave her corporate management job to become the executive director at her church. She had been in several different volunteer leadership positions, so she already knew the church's culture, its potential, and some of its challenges. Charles, the senior pastor, was also thrilled to have Sherry on board. They had developed a high level of trust during her time as a volunteer, and he knew that she brought much-needed experience. That is why he didn't hesitate to include "supervisory oversight of all the staff" as one of the key points in her job description.

In her first twelve months, Sherry put several new systems in place to improve ministry effectiveness. One of these, a new process for goal-setting and performance evaluation, was initially met with resistance. Over time, most of the staff began to understand this process and even saw that it could be a helpful tool. Except for Grant, the missions pastor. Getting members involved in missions was central to the church's vision, but Grant had demonstrated little ability to do so in his five years on staff. As Sherry worked with him, he continually made excuses for his failure to meet goals.

Sherry had kept Charles informed of these difficulties and felt that she had his full support. After Grant missed another set of milestones, Sherry told Charles that her next conversation with Grant would be to discuss an "exit strategy." She explained that she would do this gracefully, allowing him to leave with dignity and giving him time to find another position, but Charles interrupted: "I don't think that we're to that point yet. Grant really loves God, and he's done a great job with our international partners. See if you can try a different approach with him."

Sherry was exasperated. She had already tried multiple approaches. Charles had made it clear that he was unhappy with the lack of progress in missions, but she was suddenly faced with the reality that she had more responsibility than authority for this strategic priority.

I've heard Sherry's story countless times from second chair leaders. The responsibility-authority gap occurs with personnel decisions. It arises when a second chair attempts to cancel a program in order to make room for a new missional initiative, only to be overruled when an angry church member complains to the senior pastor. It occurs when the agency's executive director insists on approving every expenditure, causing decision-making to grind to a halt.

The problem of responsibility without authority is crystal clear for a second chair leader. But what about the first chair? How does this look from his perspective? Having someone who will shoulder some of the responsibility sounds great! That's why the second chair position was created. In many cases, especially when the role is new, the first chair hasn't thought about what it really means to release authority and doesn't see the consequences from failing to do so.

In Sherry's case, Charles genuinely believed that she had the authority she needed. She supervised Grant and had been fully empowered to give him direction and to discuss performance shortcomings with him. To Charles, that sounded like full authority, but to Sherry, it felt as though she was being constrained. Charles also saw this as an isolated event, but Sherry was concerned that it would be a sign to other staff members that she wasn't really their boss.

The solution, just as in the previous two sections, is a conversation between first and second chairs. When a second chair leader feels that she is being held responsible for something for which she lacks authority, she needs to bring this up with her boss. This is a more difficult conversation than the prior ones. The first chair leader may have some personal issues that cause him to hold tightly to the reins and not release authority. Of course, he may not admit this and may not even recognize it. As discussed in the previous chapter, anything that shines light on these tendencies can feel threatening.

The conversation can also be difficult because of the feedback that the second chair may receive. The central question is, "Why haven't you given me authority that is in line with my responsibilities?" While the answer may be that the first chair simply hasn't realized this mismatch, it's also possible that he doesn't have enough confidence or trust to do so. No one wants to hear this, and in many cases, the first chair doesn't even want to say it. If this is the issue, however, the only way to move toward clarity is to get it on the table.

Your first chair probably won't be so direct as to say, "I don't have confidence in you," but you can listen for clues that confidence is lacking. Phrases such as "I didn't know if you could handle that situation" or "I felt like I needed to get involved" should get your attention. That's your opportunity to ask, "Why?"

Lack of confidence isn't a dead end. It is something that can be worked on and improved. If you can understand the reasons that confidence is lacking, then you may be able to address them. Regardless of what the issues are, bringing them into the light and addressing them will begin to shrink the gap between responsibility and authority.

When Talents Are Neglected

At times, the second chair role is defined in very clear terms, and it's this clarity that is the problem. When second chair leaders feel their talents are not being used, it is frustrating. Even more so if they see ways that those abilities would directly advance the mission.

One typical version of neglected talents is when an experienced marketplace leader steps into a second chair role. It is this specific background that made the person such a great candidate for the job. During the hiring process, the first chair may have talked at length about the need for these skills and about a variety of organizational gaps that can now be addressed. But once the former businessperson crosses into the ministry world, he often finds that he's only using a portion of his expertise.

Similarly, consider the seminary-trained clergyperson who moves into the executive pastor role. Her expectation is that she will still be actively involved in ministry. And yet, it seems that most of her days are spent in meetings, in administration, and in dealing with a variety of personnel matters. Just like the businessperson, she feels that she has much to offer that is not being used.

In both cases, and others like these, the second chair feels frustrated. It's like being the best shooter on a basketball team but being told to focus on playing defense and passing the ball more often. Surely a good coach wouldn't do this, would he? Actually, he might. Perhaps it's early in the season and he has recognized some areas where this star player needs to develop in order to help the team later. Or it might have nothing to do with the star player, but instead is an attempt to develop some needed skills in others. Or the coach may know something about the team or about the next opponent that the star is unaware of. In all these cases, there may be good reasons that the star is not fully using his talents.

Of course, if the basketball player truly is a great shooter and over a long period of time finds that he's being relegated to a minor role, it may be time to look for another team. And that frames the question for second chair leaders who feel that they have talents that aren't being used. Is this just a season? Does the first chair have reasons (that you may not know) for the current division of responsibilities?

It's important that you use the gifts and abilities that God has given to you. This is a stewardship responsibility that each person must wrestle with. But before you decide that your current role doesn't adequately use those talents, engage in a conversation with your first chair. You're likely to learn something new that could change your perspective. Perhaps you'll understand that this is just a season or you'll appreciate the reason. Or the conversation may be eye-opening for your first chair, leading to a shift in your responsibilities. And even if neither of these outcomes occurs and you eventually decide to leave for a role that better suits your strengths and passions, you'll do so with fewer questions and regrets.

When Transitions Occur

You may be one of the fortunate second chair leaders for whom role clarity has never been an obstacle to your ability to thrive. For the most part, you know what's expected, you have plenty of authority, and the job plays to your strengths. That is, until a change occurs at the top of the organization. Clarity often goes out the window when the composition of the senior leadership team changes.

It is rare for a leadership team to remain unchanged over a long period of time. The team may expand from two people (e.g., senior pastor and executive pastor) to three or four, reflecting the growth of the organization or a change in leadership philosophy. Or the size may not change, but a new person may be brought onto the team when another one leaves. Any time a new person is added to a team, the dynamics change.

Regardless of the kind of change, a shift in the leadership team represents a role dis-clarifying moment for second chair leaders. Your formal job description may not change at all, and yet the nature of the role may change in a number of ways.

- Who will "all other duties" be assigned to? You may be accustomed to being the only person to whom this applies, and then a new person starts taking some of these tasks.
- How will strategic decisions be made? A new voice at the leadership table will have different perspectives and may reorder some priorities or introduce new ones.
- How will you engage in debate? A healthy team will have learned that conflict is a productive part of decision-making. With a new member, you will need to reestablish norms for disagreement.
- How will you communicate effectively? If you're moving from a two-person team to something larger, the communication challenge will grow exponentially. Offline conversations between team members are inevitable, so new patterns will be needed to keep everyone on the same page.

These are important, practical questions. But thriving through a leadership team transition really boils down to issues of ego, trust, and flexibility. You probably won't treat the new team member like an unwelcome intruder, but there are many subtle ways that ego can get in the way. You can't thrive while resenting the person who takes some of your duties or who is recognized for a great idea. It may not have been your decision to add him to the team, but it is your choice how you respond.

If trust has been high in the previous version of the team, it will take time to return to that level. You won't automatically trust the newcomer in the same way that you trusted her predecessors, and she won't fully trust you either. Communication fumbles will occur, and these can easily erode trust. So when you're wishing for the "way it used to be," realize that building trust takes time.

Of course, with a new team, it won't ever be the way it used to be. That's why flexibility is important. It's a theme that runs throughout this chapter. Clarity is helpful, but thriving second chair leaders know that they'll never have complete clarity and that they will always need to be flexible.

Nowhere is flexibility more important for second chairs than when the church or ministry experiences a transition in first chair leaders. The simple truth is that a transition in first chairs often leads to a transition in second chairs. Sometimes this is appropriate. I vividly remember a highly respected, long-tenured executive pastor telling me, "I have no pretensions that I'd be the right second chair for a different senior pastor."

That perspective is powerful in a transition. "I might not be the right second chair for this new first chair." The statement is not a reflection on the second chair's past contributions or current gifts. The second chair may have played a key role in implementing a bold vision and may have incredible leadership ability, but might not be the right "fit" for the incoming leader. The statement is not a prediction of the outcome either. "Might not" is a recognition that things have changed. It's an acceptance that there needs to be a period of evaluation. But it's not a pronouncement about the future.

The only way to find out if you're the "right second chair" is to spend time to see if you can "dance together." If you're faced with a transition, how should you try to dance with a new first chair?

- *Be patient.* If you had a great partnership with the previous first chair, it's unrealistic to expect this from the start. It took years for you to develop that level of trust and chemistry, so give the new relationship time.

- *Lead less.* This advice may seem counterintuitive. After all, you have the tenure and credibility to step up and provide leadership while the newcomer is adjusting. You may have done this during an interim period. Just realize that the new first chair wants to establish leadership and may feel insecure or overshadowed if you take too much initiative.
- *Communicate more.* Perhaps the former relationship was so smooth that you could almost read each other's minds. As a result, you didn't have to think much about communication. With a new first chair, you need to be much more intentional and proactive in your communications. This is one of the best ways to build a trusting relationship and to learn his personality and leadership style, which is knowledge that will enable you to thrive in the future.

Role clarity is like a clear spring for second chairs who want to thrive, but this doesn't mean that the role will be completely predictable or unchanging. Earlier in this chapter, I used the analogy of a basketball team, but a better sports analogy for second chair leaders comes from soccer. If you've ever watched a World Cup game, you have probably noticed that there are times when the players don't seem to be in their assigned positions. In the flow of the game, a defender may rush forward into an offensive position, and a midfielder may step back to cover the gap in the defense. It's not that they've forgotten their roles. In fact, this fluidity is exactly what needs to happen in order for the team to win. As you perform "all other duties" in the second chair, remember that your team's success depends on you embracing this duality of knowing your role and demonstrating the same kind of flexibility.

Personal Reflection

- Which of the role-clarity challenges are you dealing with (see pages 36–38)?
- Are your expectations for clarity realistic, given what you know about your first chair and the church or ministry? Have you accepted that a certain amount of flexibility will always be needed? Is any part of the clarity challenge due to your own unrealistic expectations?
- Is your first chair aware of your concerns about role clarity?
- Has your team experienced a recent transition? If so, how is that affecting you?

Discuss with Your First Chair

- Discuss areas where the second chair's role is not clear or where he or she is feeling frustrated (e.g., unrealistic expectations, not using his or her gifts).
- Second chairs: Remember that your first chair sees the organization from a different vantage point. Ask him or her to share that perspective regarding your role.
- First chairs: If the conversation about role clarity makes you think that your second chair needs to be more flexible, talk with him or her about this.

Chapter 4

Think (and Act) Strategically

Second chairs who thrive focus on the most important priorities by seeing the big picture and making decisions in light of this.

If you ask a second chair leader what he or she "does," you may hear a long list of tasks. These include managing and developing staff, creating systems for more effective ministry, and working with leadership teams (topics that are covered in the next three chapters), along with a variety of special projects. But if you ask about their greatest contribution to the organization, and give them a minute to reflect, their answer will typically point to their ability to think and act strategically.

This is not to suggest that you need to have an MBA or be a strategic planning expert to be an effective second chair leader. Nor does it imply that second chairs carry the primary responsibility for discerning the overall vision for their church or ministry. But it does mean that effective second chair leaders operate with a time horizon that is longer than today. They are making decisions based on the bigger picture. They are looking ahead, trying to prepare for the future and anticipate obstacles that could impede the organization's progress.

What Is "Strategic Thinking"?

If you are not a born strategist, this description may be too vague or philosophical. You may know that someone on your leadership team needs to think and act strategically, but you are looking for a more concrete understanding of how to do this. Let me offer four phrases to paint that picture.

Thinking strategically means *adding value throughout the organization*. This is a key phrase from our original definition of a second chair leader. It is what separates the second chair from other roles that are more narrowly focused on a specific area of ministry. Strategic thinking asks the question, "How can we best make progress toward our God-given vision?" To effectively answer this question, you must consider the bigger picture that spans the entire church or ministry and that looks over the next several months or years. "Adding value throughout" is a mind-set, not a specific job title. Even someone who has functional responsibility for an individual department can have organization-wide impact by thinking strategically.

When second chair leaders are thinking strategically, they act as *leaders, not managers*. Warren Bennis and Burt Nanus coined this often-repeated distinction, explaining, "Managers are people who do things right and leaders are people who do the right things."[1] A manager, in this framework, tends to stay within the boundaries and follow established procedures. Leaders, on the other hand, will challenge those boundaries and procedures if they see a better way to accomplish the mission. Leaders are not content with the status quo. But effective leaders don't make change just for the sake of shaking things up. They do so with the long-term mission in mind. An organization needs both, and second chairs often must function as managers, but strategic thinking calls for them to wear a leader's hat at least some of the time.

This kind of thinking requires a second chair to *spend time above the weeds and below the clouds*. Most second chair leaders spend at least part of their time working on detailed, short-term issues. But if all of your time is spent in these "weeds," it's impossible to be strategic. It is equally unproductive to spend all of your time "in the clouds," thinking about the highest level of vision. This may happen because it's where a visionary leader likes to live or because a leadership team has developed a habit of pontificating but not making practical decisions. High-level vision is important, but you can't be effective if you never come down below the clouds.

The space between clouds and weeds is the realm of strategy. A church may have a vision to be the resource of choice for families in its community. But what kind of family or need do they have in mind? What specific programs will they offer? Will they partner with other churches or agencies? These are the kinds of strategic questions that must be answered to move toward the vision. They should

1. Warren Bennis and Burt Nanus, *Leaders: The Strategies for Taking Charge* (New York: HarperCollins, 1985), 21.

not be confused with "weedy," tactical questions such as space requirements for one of the programs or job descriptions for the person leading the ministry.

That leads to the final phrase: *giving feet to the vision*. One of the hallmarks of second chairs who think strategically is that their churches and ministries are not stagnant. They are moving toward a vision with intentionality. They are setting priorities and allocating resources based on their understanding of how they can best achieve the vision. As my friend Jim Neikirk says, "A decision hasn't been made until resources have been committed." In this respect, these second chair leaders are not just thinking strategically, they are acting strategically.

Karen's circuitous path to second chair leadership began when she was an agnostic, sitting on the fringe of a neighborhood Bible study. Within a year, she had become one of the founding members of City Church and had discovered that her musical gifts could be used in worship. After starting as a volunteer on the worship team, she eventually became a part-time worship leader, and then the full-time director of worship. Matt, the senior pastor and leader of that original home Bible study, encouraged Karen to use her leadership gifts. As the church grew, he asked her to join the newly formed executive team and oversee all of the church's ministries.

Karen embraced her new role and the opportunity to help Matt and the church live into the vision of "partnering with God to bring about lasting life transformation for people in the community." During her first several months in the second chair role, Karen intentionally set aside times to evaluate everything that City Church was doing in light of its vision. She was excited about a variety of things, including the number of new people coming into the church. But she was discouraged when she discovered that almost half of the new members had left the church within two years. This hardly seemed like "lasting life transformation."

This realization prompted a number of difficult discussions within the executive team and the broader staff. Karen was gentle in not allowing the conversation to become a blame game, but she insisted that they be honest about the problem and seek to uncover the underlying issues. After several lengthy meetings, they developed a multi-pronged plan to help City Church's newest members connect more deeply. The plan required reallocation of resources, including some modest cuts in the worship budget. While this step was difficult for Karen, especially given her history and passion for worship, she knew that it was the right thing to do.

Habits of Strategic Thinkers

You may already have plenty of opportunities to be strategic, just like Karen. But if not, you may be wondering how to start. Karen's story, and a variety of others like hers, highlights four foundational habits. Second chair leaders who think and act strategically unpack the vision, evaluate honestly, plan the steps, and move to the balcony.

Unpack the Vision

Karen had a tremendous advantage over many second chair leaders—she had a crystal-clear understanding of the vision. She had known Matt before City Church launched, and she had been involved in the church's leadership from its earliest days. The vision of "lasting life transformation for people in the community" wasn't just a phrase to her. She had personally experienced it and had heard Matt communicate this vision in a variety of ways. She had heard him explain it to other leaders and to newcomers to the church. She had been part of lengthy discussions about what the vision meant and how to achieve it.

If the vision is fuzzy, it is virtually impossible for a second chair to think strategically. The importance of clarifying vision has already been discussed in chapters 1 and 2, but it is worth restating here because of its impact on strategic decision-making. I could have a "vision" of a family vacation to California. I'm sure that my family would be excited about the trip, but they would want to know more about my "vision." Are we going to Los Angeles? San Francisco? Yosemite? Are we going in the summer or winter? How long will we be gone? The answers to these questions will make all the difference in how they prepare for the trip. And if we can't answer these questions, we won't go anywhere at all.

Second chair leaders have a crucial role to play when the vision is vague. They are the ones who most readily see the places where clarity is lacking. They are the ones who have (or should have) trust-based relationships with first chairs that make it possible to discuss points that are confusing. And they are the ones who can work with the first chair and other leaders to unpack the vision and produce greater understanding.

Unpacking the vision requires asking questions. This is true even if you have recently been through some kind of visioning process. Questions such as, "What do we mean when we say 'lasting life transformation'?" or "If we do ______, does that align with our vision?" One of my favorites is: "If we do nothing else, what one major change or initiative must we pursue?" This question brings clarity to vision and surfaces true priorities. These questions should not be threatening. In truth, they are an essential part of unpacking the vision and are absolutely necessary for strategic thinking.

The leaders of one church knew that they had a space problem, but they were unsure how to address it. Then an opportunity to purchase space for a second campus fell into their laps. A real estate developer in the church was willing to sell a building to them for much less than market value, so the church didn't hesitate. Over the next several months, as they worked on plans for the building renovation, they also developed ministry plans for the shift to multisite. But everything was put on hold when they were approached by a company that offered to pay almost double the original purchase price for the new building. Kyle, the executive pastor, knew that this was not just a transaction. It was an opportunity to unpack a vision that had been too vague.

Kyle organized a retreat for the executive staff and elders during which they prayerfully asked whether their vision called for them to be a multisite church. In deciding that the answer to this question was "yes," they also clarified the style of multisite church that they were called to be and realized that the specific building was not central to that vision. The church took the offer and used the profit to accelerate their strategy.

As you think about your church or ministry's vision, you may feel confused like Kyle rather than clear like Karen. If that's the case, don't give up on strategic thinking as a means of thriving. Sometimes the most important step in thinking strategically is unpacking the vision so that you can decide what is strategic.

Evaluate Honestly

Thinking strategically means making decisions that will have a major impact on the church or ministry's future. It may be a decision to sell a piece of property or launch a new ministry or cancel a program. These kinds of decisions should not be made on a whim, but only through prayer *and* informed evaluation.

In *Good to Great,* Jim Collins says that great leaders "confront the brutal facts."[2] They don't run from information that paints a negative picture. They recognize that ignoring facts might avoid temporary discomfort but will ultimately lead to much worse long-term outcomes. An honest evaluation of what is working, and what is not, is a powerful tool for second chair leaders who are striving

2. Jim Collins, *Good to Great: Why Some Companies Make the Leap... and Others Don't* (New York: HarperCollins, 2001), 65.

to think strategically. It is what enabled Karen to start the conversation that led to the major shifts at City Church.

Notice that Collins says leaders "confront the brutal facts," not that they are brutal in how they use facts. This can be a point of confusion in Christian settings. Some church and ministry leaders shy away from looking closely at data because they're afraid that someone will be offended. They think that assessment always leads to blame. It is possible, however, to conduct an evaluation for the purpose of learning and improving, not for labeling someone as a failure. And even if a person's feelings get hurt, that may be a small price to pay compared to the poor stewardship of making an unwise strategic decision.

Several years ago, the Reveal survey at Willow Creek Community Church made headlines in ministry circles. The extensive survey of the church's members was designed to identify what activities and emphases best promoted spiritual growth. It *revealed* that the traditional mind-set of getting people to do more—more small groups, Bible studies, serving opportunities—was not a primary driver of spiritual development. It might have been tempting for Willow Creek's leadership to bury the results of this survey. After all, it indicated that many of their efforts had been less effective than they had thought. But instead, the church's leaders used this information to dramatically reshape their approach to discipleship.

Willow Creek's experience with Reveal shows another important dimension of honest evaluation—the need to dive deep. The superficial data that is most readily available for churches and ministries does not allow for meaningful assessments. Willow Creek used an extensive survey to take a deeper look. At City Church, the average worship attendance was growing. It was only when Karen looked more closely at the data that she identified a problem. If an issue is truly strategic, it calls for an in-depth evaluation.

Up to this point, "evaluate honestly" has been described in a retrospective sense, looking back at what has or hasn't worked. The same mind-set, however, can be used to look forward. When a leadership team is considering different options—whether that is the next initiative or staff hire or facility upgrade—they should also evaluate deeply and honestly. They should ask, "In light of our vision, which of the various paths do we believe will produce the greatest fruit? Why do we believe this? What evidence do we have to support this belief?" Once an honest, in-depth evaluation has been done, a second chair can move to the next habit, planning the steps that need to be taken.

Plan the Steps

The heart of thinking and acting strategically is putting together the plans to move a church or ministry toward its vision. It's what happens between the clouds and the weeds. It is one of the most powerful ways that a second chair leader complements a visionary first chair.

My friend Phil Taylor says, "Many Lead Pastors . . . have little knowledge or passion for how you go about actually taking a vision from step 1 to step 100. Steps 2 through 99 are kind of boring to them."[3] Even if those intervening steps aren't "boring" to a first chair, it takes time and effort to figure them out, and that time is a precious resource for any leader.

On the opposite end of the spectrum you will find members of the staff who can't see beyond step 2. They're deep in the weeds, trying to make sure that everyone understands steps 1(a), 1(b), 1(c), and maybe even 1(a)(i) and 1(a)(ii). The steps beyond number 2 are almost incomprehensible, not boring, for them. Even if they recognize the existence of those later steps, they have difficulty thinking about them as long as the immediate details are unsettled.

In between these extremes is where second chairs can add immeasurable value by thinking strategically. They may be able to convince the first chair to slow down and wrestle with key decisions related to steps 2 through 98. Or they may be trusted to make these decisions with minimal input from the first chair. They can invite the detail-oriented staff members into the planning conversation, helping them think beyond step 2 and then releasing them to work out the other intricacies.

Once City Church's executive team agreed that the loss of new members was a strategic priority, the ball was in Karen's court to develop a plan. She worked with a small team of staff members and lay leaders to better understand the problem and identify possible solutions. The final plan included changes in the content for the new member class, greater emphasis on getting new members into small groups, a yearlong small group for people who were new believers, and hiring a part-time staff person to oversee the implementation of these plans. They also began generating reports from the church database to give the leadership better and more timely information in order to evaluate results and make adjustments as necessary.

Thinking and acting strategically does not mean that second chair leaders will never have to involve themselves in mundane activities. There will always

3. Phil Taylor, *Defining the Executive Pastor Role* (Orlando: Floodlight Press, 2015), 25.

be times when you have to dive into details, whether responding to a crisis or insuring implementation. But when you're staying strategic, even those less-than-exhilarating activities take on a different meaning. Designing the new report on member retention is not strategic by itself, but it may be a critical step that needs a second chair's input. It's connecting the dots between the details and the vision, and that is a strategic activity.

Move to the Balcony

The final foundational habit—moving to the balcony—is certainly not the last one to be done. In fact, it needs to be practiced regularly in a second chair's life. The benefit that a leader gains from spending time on the balcony is described in Ron Heifetz's *Leadership Without Easy Answers*.[4] He uses the image of a formal ball with a crowded dance floor. A person who stays on the ground floor will be caught up in the swirl of the dance, constantly bumping into others and seeing little of what's happening in the room. If that person moves to the balcony, he will be able to see much more of the ball. What's informative in this illustration is that nothing has changed except for the individual's perspective.

The previous three habits—understanding vision, evaluating honestly, and planning the steps—require that second chair leaders have this kind of big-picture perspective. By moving to the balcony, Karen was able to assess City Church's retention problem. If she had stayed on the "dance floor," she probably would have "bumped into" this issue. She would have also bumped into many others—a staff member who felt unfairly treated by his boss, a conflict between two groups that both wanted to use the same meeting space, the communications director who was frustrated by missed deadlines.

The biggest obstacle to strategic thinking for second chair leaders isn't a lack of aptitude or the complexity of the problem or a difficult first chair leader. The biggest obstacle is not taking the time to move to the balcony. Effective strategic thinking cannot be done in the two-minute breaks between meetings or in the thirty minutes at the end of the day when everyone else has left but when most of your energy and creativity is also gone. It requires blocking out time when you're at your best so that you can work on the matters that are most important.

As easy as this is to say, I know that it's difficult to do. The people and problems on the dance floor don't just bump into the second chair leader who is

4. Ronald A. Heifetz, *Leadership without Easy Answers* (Cambridge: Harvard University Press, 1998), 253.

trying to move to the balcony—they seem to grab the leader by the shoulders, refusing to let go. Second chair leaders find it particularly difficult to escape this grip because part of their job is to keep these issues from reaching the first chair. They know that the unhappy staff member or the space usage conflict won't go away, and might actually get worse if they don't address it.

Tony's church was at the size where they needed an executive pastor, but they could only afford to have this position if the person also had some direct ministry responsibilities. Tony gladly threw himself into the specific ministry areas and the broader leadership that his second chair role demanded. A year later, Tony met with his senior pastor, Grace, to review his performance and his goals for the coming year. She was thrilled with how much he had accomplished, but she was concerned about his goals. As the conversation unfolded, Grace explained, "Tony, I'd actually like you to have fewer goals next year. The greatest value that you bring to me and to this church is when you step away and work on the bigger picture issues."

While I can't make it easy to move to the balcony, let me at least point the way to the stairs that can take you there. One of the best practices is to proactively schedule time on your calendar for strategic thinking. Block out a half day (or a full day) to wrestle with one or more strategic questions that are facing your church or ministry. Put those times on the calendar far enough in advance so that there's still some white space around them, and then protect them unless you have a genuine emergency.

In most cases, you should plan to spend that time away from the office. Staff members who wouldn't dare disturb a first chair don't hesitate to knock on the door of the second chair to "interrupt for just a quick second." That "quick second" typically turns into a fifteen-minute conversation (or longer), plus the added time to gather your thoughts and get back on track. Your team needs to understand the importance of this balcony time. You're not taking time off, running errands, or pursuing some trivial task. The time that you're spending to think strategically is arguably the most valuable way to invest that half day. If they understand this and if they feel empowered, some of those dance floor bumps may get resolved without your help.

If you look ahead on your calendar and you can't find time for a half day of strategic thinking, then you may be dealing with another issue. You may have become the victim of your own effectiveness, with too many responsibilities being piled on your plate. It may be time for you to have a conversation with your first chair about delegating some of those duties, a topic we'll come back to in chapter 10.

Up to this point, I've made it sound as though moving to the balcony is a solo endeavor. And while there are times when you need to get away on your own, it's often appropriate and even more helpful to invite others to the balcony with you. Include your first chair leader if you need to unpack the vision or address a specific issue that he is passionate about. Bring the executive team or some other leadership group to the balcony at other times. As you all look out on that crowded dance floor, they will see things that you've failed to notice. They will have new ideas that haven't occurred to you. And they will also learn the value of spending time on the balcony.

A Strategic Role

Before you run up to the balcony and dive into your church or ministry's important strategic questions, let me encourage you to go back to the issue of role clarity (chapter 3). In many ways, a second chair leader's responsibility relative to the organization's strategy is the hardest part of the role to define. It is difficult to say, "This is where vision ends and strategy begins," and it can also be difficult to articulate where the line is drawn between first and second chairs in their responsibilities for strategic thinking. The truth is that both need to be involved, but they need to do so in a way that doesn't cause conflict between them or confusion for others.

Second chair leaders should not make assumptions about the degree of authority that they have in this arena. Instead, they should clarify the expectations of their first chairs. A few key questions are:

- If the vision isn't clear to me, what's the best way to gain a better understanding?
- How much do you want to be involved in developing the strategies? How much freedom do I have in this?
- If I have a fair amount of freedom, how should I keep you in the loop? What's important for you to know?
- If you're staying highly involved in developing strategies, what is my role? How do you want me to support you?

The perspective throughout this chapter is that thinking strategically is a key part of a second chair leader's job. But what if that kind of big-picture thinking doesn't come easily for you? It's possible that you're in the wrong role. More likely, though, you will need to lean more on others to help you think strategically. The "other" person might be your first chair or another member of the leadership team or a key volunteer. Don't be afraid to ask for help—your church or ministry needs the benefit of strategic thinking, and you may grow in your abilities as you learn from others.

I could write much more about strategic thinking. In fact, I have. The next three chapters focus on different aspects of the second chair role—managing people, creating structure and process, and interacting with governance bodies. Any of these three could consume every waking minute of a second chair's day. That's why an underpinning of all three is that thriving second chair leaders think strategically in deciding where and how to invest their time and energy. Take that thought to the balcony as you explore the next three springs for thriving.

Personal Reflection

- This chapter began with several phrases that describe "strategic thinking." In what ways is this either a strength or an area for growth?
- Is the overall vision of your church/ministry clear enough for you to develop strategies?
- Do you evaluate routinely? What changes do you need to make in order to evaluate more effectively?
- How often do you get to the balcony? Schedule your next balcony time right now.

Discuss with Your First Chair

- What are the strategic priorities that flow out of the vision? If the two of you have different answers for this question, does the vision need to be clarified?
- What is the second chair's role/authority for developing strategies and goals for the church or ministry? How does the first chair want to be involved in these decisions?
- How much balcony time do the two of you need to spend together? What's the best way to do this?

Chapter 5

Develop for the Future

Second chairs who thrive view supervision as an opportunity to coach and develop staff members toward success, even when facing difficult situations.

"I'm looking forward to a season when I'm not dealing with personnel issues." Those words, spoken by the executive pastor of a large church, still ring in my ears, even though that was years ago. I also remember my response: "This might not be the right role for you."

My answer may have been too blunt, but I believe the message was correct. Second chair leaders generally carry a heavy responsibility related to staff. They are involved in hiring, training, developing, evaluating, promoting, reprimanding, rewarding, and firing. In smaller churches, some of these duties may apply to volunteers or be carried out by volunteers who function as second chairs. Even if the management responsibility is shared with a first chair leader or others, the second chair can't escape this "burden." Hence my response.

But does the management of staff and volunteers have to be a burden? It will never be easy to tell someone that their performance isn't meeting expectations or to terminate a staff member. Someone will always be asking for special treatment or expressing dissatisfaction. If you want to thrive, you will understand that these are small but necessary parts of the job, and you will rejoice in the many victories that come as you develop staff members to live into their God-given potential.

Chapter 5

It's Complicated

When it comes to staff management, do you tend to land on the side of grace or stewardship? Grace emphasizes forgiveness and second chances when someone fails to meet performance expectations. Stewardship holds a much firmer line, arguing that resources are being wasted when performance deficiencies are ignored.

The best leaders live in this tension and strive to achieve "both/and." They give second chances, but they don't give second chances for the fifth time. They understand that leaving someone in a position where they are floundering is not compassionate. They also understand that they have a stewardship responsibility, not just for financial resources but also for helping staff members develop their gifts and succeed in their roles.

Practicing the both/and of grace plus stewardship is complicated. If you entered the second chair from the corporate arena, you may have a distinct advantage relative to many of your colleagues. Your former company may have done a great job in hiring and developing people. They may have been very fair and consistent in addressing performance problems. But before you try to copy all of those practices, realize that you also have a distinct disadvantage. Personnel matters in ministry settings are almost always more complicated than in business.

Several years ago, I had the opportunity to hear the head of human resources from a large nonprofit organization address a group of executive pastors. She offered a number of helpful and practical insights, but much of it went out the window during the question-and-answer time at the end. One of the executive pastors asked for advice on how to deal with a staff member who was chronically late for work. The executive pastor knew that the employee had been having some marital difficulties that contributed to the tardiness. She suspected that things at home had worsened and wondered the best way to be pastoral while also addressing the problem. The HR expert was quick and to the point: "You can't be pastor and manager. Focus on the performance issue, and if it doesn't improve, start the formal disciplinary process."

In that moment, the entire group seemed to disengage. While this answer may have been correct in a textbook sense, it seemed completely unrealistic. What kind of church or ministry wouldn't care about the lives of staff members? The moment that you care, however, ministry gets complicated. It is complicated when a long-time church member applies for a job and meets some, but not all, of the requirements. It's complicated when a staff member who was a star performer doesn't have the skills to go to the next level as the church grows. And it's certainly complicated when you try to evaluate "effectiveness" for something that is inherently hard to assess, such as the quality of pastoral care.

The "First" Complication

One of the most complicated dynamics is when first and second chair leaders don't see eye-to-eye on personnel matters. The issue may be a hiring decision or a promotion or a termination. Regardless of the specifics, these can be some of the most troublesome differences to resolve.

The difficulty starts with the bi-modal and subjective nature of many personnel issues. "Bi-modal" refers to the fact that many of these decisions seem to only have two options. The person will or won't be hired. The same with promotions or terminations. The first chair may land on one side and the second chair on the other. On both sides, their reasoning is largely subjective. One sees no issues with "culture fit" (or attitude, leadership capacity, and so forth) and the other sees major red flags. This creates a situation that is tense and seems unresolvable.

One of Ruth's first decisions as senior pastor was to promote the children's director into a campus pastor role. This decision was well received, but it didn't take long before parents began expressing their anxiety about the vacancy. Even though a good interim team was in place, Ruth felt pressured to find a great new children's director quickly. Mark, the executive pastor, had the official responsibility of leading an ad hoc team to conduct this search, but Ruth stayed involved. When she was given the name of a promising candidate named Monica, she immediately gave her a call. They established an instant rapport, which Ruth reported to Mark. Over the next three weeks, Ruth pushed Mark to move the search along, and she eventually started advocating directly for Monica. Mark was concerned that Monica's former senior pastor had given a less-than-glowing reference. Ruth was sure that this was just a "chemistry" issue. Eventually, Mark relented and led the team to hire Monica. A few months later Mark was dealing with the consequences of a less-than-effective hire.

Second chair leaders generally lose if they get locked into a bi-modal argument with their first chair. The first chair may play the "I'm the boss" trump card to make the decision. Or the second chair may push hard enough to "win" the argument but damage the relationship in the process. That's why it is valuable to escape from bi-modal thinking whenever possible. Can the person be hired first as a temp or with a clear probationary time period? Can the promotion be given, but with less responsibility for the first six months?

One of the reasons for this divide is that the second chair leader is often more concerned about living with the consequences of poor personnel decisions. The first chair says, "I'm sure it will work out." The second chair thinks, *But I'm the one paying the cost for how it "works out."* The specific cost may be dealing with turmoil caused by promoting someone who doesn't lead effectively or hiring a "nice" church member who lacks the skills for the job. The cost may be large or small, but either way, it's a cost that second chairs would rather not pay.

The root of this divide is that many first chair leaders land on the side of grace while many second chairs lean toward stewardship. In addition to the tension between these two, it can lead staff to play the game of "Dad said no, so let's go ask Mom." On the positive side, these differing perspectives can lead to better decisions and help each leader discover the "both/and" of grace and stewardship described above. This will only happen if their relationship is healthy and if they are committed to staying in dialogue.

Other Complications

Even if the first and second chair leaders have learned to leverage their differences in positive ways for managing staff, other complications can threaten a second chair's ability to thrive. Sandra had been in the executive pastor role for three years and continued to be surprised at how much time she spent on staff-related issues. There was the music director who wanted an exception to the nepotism policy so that he could hire his wife as organist. Then there was the assistant director in the youth ministry, whose performance had been inadequate for three years but who had never received a performance review. After that was the incident with the campus pastor who had created his own mission initiative rather than supporting the one that was intended to be church-wide. As Sandra reflected back on these incidents, she realized that she was constantly dealing with "special cases."

Sandra's story illustrates the kind of complications that many second chairs face when managing staff. Four major categories are:

- *Lack of systems.* A variety of systems are needed in order for staff management and development to function effectively. Most churches and ministries are far behind where they need to be in creating and using these systems. When the shortcomings affect the ability to attract and retain high-quality staff, the impact on the second chair is significant. (More on this in chapter 6.)

- *Unclear criteria.* "Criteria" includes the expectations for a role, the qualifications for a new hire, and the definition of excellent performance. When a church or ministry fails to clarify the criteria in any of these or other personnel-related areas, it hampers the second chair's ability to manage staff effectively.
- *Inadequate training.* Some second chair leaders have not received formal or informal training in staff management. They may also be supervising staff who lack this kind of training. This may not seem to be a problem, until a problem arises, and then they suddenly feel unprepared.
- *Too many "chiefs."* A common frustration for second chairs is when the first chair contradicts a decision related to personnel. But the first chair is not the only person who can cause confusion. A variety of other people (church members, ministry board members or constituents) may feel the freedom to intervene in staff matters. They may complain about perceived performance issues, lobby for a promotion, or question a reprimand.

Conner was new in the second chair role at the largest local outreach ministry in the city, but he was not new to management. Conner's clear articulation of a coaching philosophy for managing staff was one of the primary reasons that the executive director and board decided to hire him. When he arrived, he discovered that none of his direct reports had job descriptions or annual goals, nor had they received any kind of formal performance feedback over the previous two years. Conner wanted to help each of them grow, but he had no basis for knowing where growth was most needed. Over the next few months, several board members suggested improvement needs for different staff members, but these ideas were often contradictory. At his six-month anniversary, Conner went to lunch with his boss. His first words were, "I'm not sure what I've gotten myself into."

Making the Shift(s)

Perhaps you feel like Conner. You may be new to the second chair role and may have even said, "I'm not sure what I've gotten myself into." Or perhaps you're a more seasoned second chair who has a pretty good idea of what you've gotten into. The better question is, "How can I get out of this mess?" This isn't a question about how to exit your job, but rather asks what changes need to be made in order for you and your church or ministry to thrive.

If personnel-related challenges are one of your biggest obstacles to thriving, there are five shifts that you should consider making. These shifts involve different ways of *acting* and *thinking*. They don't ignore the reality that personnel matters can be messy, especially in ministry settings, but they move toward positive ways of dealing with the messiness. In order to thrive in the second chair, you need to shift from:

- special cases to effective systems,
- task-orientation to relational emphasis,
- wishful thinking to intentionality,
- confrontation to conversation,
- supervising to coaching.

From Special Cases to Effective Systems

I began this chapter with an assertion that second chair leaders will always have personnel matters to address. But as demonstrated in the earlier story of Sandra, the amount of time and energy (and frustration) expended to address these matters grows exponentially if every situation is a "special case."

Special cases come in two varieties. The first is when there are no systems or policies. In these cases, it feels as though you are making it up as you go. These situations are often made more complex when the triggering event is a crisis that requires a quick decision.

A valued administrative assistant is about to come back from maternity leave, and asks to work from home two days a week. She hints that she might quit if her request is denied. This has never been done before and you don't have a policy in place. What answer should you give?

The second category of special cases occurs when a request is made for an exception to an established policy or system. In the case of the administrative assistant, there may be a policy that prohibits working from home as a regular practice. That doesn't prevent her from making the request, nor does it keep her direct supervisor from lobbying for an exception.

I am not naïve about this issue. Even "well managed" churches and ministries make exceptions and have personnel issues that aren't covered by their policies. I am not suggesting that faith-based organizations should adopt the complex and rigid approaches to human resources that can be found in some large corporate environments. But as described further in the next chapter, the *right* systems for personnel can be a strategic asset for advancing the mission. There is great value in having effective systems to get the right people on board and point them in the right direction.

Effective systems can also minimize the unintended consequences that often occur in special cases. No decision is made in isolation—there will always be a ripple effect. If one administrative assistant is allowed to work at home two days a week, others may make similar requests. If these requests are not approved, tensions may arise. If they are approved, you may be surprised to find that no one is available in the office to help with a special project one day.

Shifting toward systems and away from special cases has a further personal benefit for second chair leaders. It reduces the amount of time that they spend on personnel issues. If you have a standard process for hiring, then you don't need multiple meetings just to decide how to handle a specific opening. If you have a system for performance reviews, it will take much less time than if you are creating something new each year.

From a Task-Orientation to a Relational Emphasis

Some of you are already highly relational and don't need to make any shifts here. You naturally focus first on people. But for many others, whether due to your internal wiring or the nature of the role, the pile of tasks to be done is the first mountain you climb.

This shouldn't be surprising. I rarely meet a second chair leader who doesn't feel swamped by the length of his or her "to do" list. While second chair roles vary widely, one of the common denominators is the importance of execution and the ability to get things done. This simple phrase—"get things done"—underscores a perennial challenge. "Things" can easily take precedent over people. When that happens, people feel undervalued and it becomes more difficult to accomplish the priority "things."

In their best-selling book *First, Break All the Rules*, Marcus Buckingham and Curt Coffman identify the questions that best predict employee engagement. Satisfaction and engagement can make a world of difference in your church or ministry. Think of the impact that an enthusiastic staff member can have in connecting with potential members compared to one with a lukewarm attitude. Think of the quality of teaching that comes from a highly engaged youth ministry leader versus one who serves out of habit or obligation.

According to Buckingham and Coffman's research, two of the top six questions for predicting satisfaction and engagement are: "Does my supervisor, or someone at work, seem to care about me as a person?" and "Is there someone at work who encourages my development?"[1] This research, and that of many others, is clear. If you want to get things done, you need to demonstrate that people are more important than things.

During my first coaching session with Marty, the word *output* came up several times in reference to the effectiveness of different staff members. It became clear that producing a large quantity of high-quality work was one of the ministry's unspoken values. As our conversations continued over the next several months, it was no surprise that there were a number of strained relationships and frustrated individuals on staff. It was an environment where everyone knew that the quality of relationships was secondary to producing great work.

If you're feeling a twinge of guilt or discomfort at this point, I am not about to ask you to undergo a complete personality change. That would be as effective as asking a leopard to change its spots. But I will offer some simple suggestions that can help you shift toward a greater relational emphasis.

Conduct a mental audit of your interactions with staff members, especially those who report directly to you. How often do you meet with them when you don't have a specific agenda? This could be a regular lunch or something less formal such as stopping in a different person's office each day just to check in.

As you continue your audit, reflect on how well you know those staff members. Do you know their stories? Do you know the things they are currently celebrating and the burdens they are carrying? One of the positive aspects of working in a church or ministry setting is that there are no restrictions on praying for and with our colleagues. So take advantage of this and demonstrate that you truly care for the people who work with you and for you.

An awareness of professional growth needs is another aspect of knowing staff and putting relationships first. What have you done to encourage the development of each of your direct reports in the last month? This may be giving them the time or funding to attend a training event, but it can also be less structured.

1. Marcus Buckingham and Curt Coffman, *First, Break All the Rules: What the World's Greatest Managers Do Differently* (New York: Simon & Schuster, 1999), 34.

Spend extra time with a new staff person to make sure that he is getting acclimated to the culture. Give one of your managers the responsibility for a special project that will help her develop some new skills, and make sure she feels the freedom to take some risks. Invite a junior person into a leadership meeting to observe and learn how decisions are made. These kinds of informal development steps can be quite meaningful for staff and effective for their growth.

From Wishful Thinking to Intentionality

How often have you been in a conversation about a personnel-related issue that has been centered in wishful thinking? "If we just give our program director a little more time, she will get more organized." "It's just a busy season, so I'm sure that the workload for the financial office will be more manageable soon." Wishful thinking often flows out of an over-emphasis on relationship and grace that neglects stewardship.

Statements like these may be accurate. The program director may get more organized. It may just be a busy season for the financial office. But often, the statements are simply a way to postpone a more difficult conversation. We may have hired the wrong person for the program director position. We may need to add a person in the financial office.

The shift toward greater intentionality starts with determining whether you are dealing with wishful thinking. A simple question can shed light on this: What leads us to believe that this statement is true? The program director may have been very organized in a previous job. The financial office may be closing the fiscal year and preparing for an audit. If the answer, however, sounds like, "I just think it's going to get better," then you're probably dealing with wishes more than reality.

Sometimes it isn't clear whether you're dealing with wishful thinking. When this is the case, ask two other questions: How soon can we expect to see improvement? What would be the indicators that we've turned the corner on this issue? These questions accept the explanation that a situation is temporary, but they also establish a timeline for progress. If the timeline isn't met, then it's time for a different conversation.

Intentionality doesn't mean being the bad guy or the gloomy doomsayer. It does mean saying, "I think we have an important issue here that's not going away on its own. Can we discuss it and try to come up with a solution?" The solution may be training or administrative support for the program director. It may be a part-time person for the financial office.

When Jake was hired to fill the new director of welcoming position, Rusti (the executive pastor) explained to him, "We need someone who will help us get better organized in this area and who will lead the way in connecting with people who are visiting the church." Jake had done an excellent job of the former, creating new processes that greatly improved the church's interactions with guests. But after a year on the job, Rusti was concerned about the latter. At first, she assumed that Jake was swamped with the challenge of addressing the organizational gaps. Eventually she began to wonder if there was a deeper reason. Over the course of several meetings, it became clear that Jake was worried about "saying the wrong thing" that might push a visitor away from the church, so his solution was to avoid the conversations completely. Without Rusti's intentionality, the issue could have been put on the back burner indefinitely.

The shift to intentionality is supported by a shift from *ideas to accountability*. Ministry leaders are often full of ideas. An animated brainstorming session may generate new and creative ways to expand a ministry or address a problem. But in the months after the brainstorming, will those ideas translate into action? Often the answer is "no." Great ideas aren't enough. Before the meeting ends, the decision on which ideas to pursue needs to be made, and responsibilities and deadlines need to be assigned. Second chairs are typically the ones who insure that this happens and hold people accountable for those assignments.

Shifting from wishful thinking to greater intentionality isn't easy. In the moment, it's almost always less painful to accept wishful thinking. In the long run, however, wishful thinking allows a problem to grow, which forces a more difficult conversation down the road. Intentionality can nip that problem in the bud. Is it time for you to shift away from wishful thinking?

From Confrontation to Conversation

It's easy to be relational and intentional when a staff member is performing well. But what about those times when they are not meeting expectations? Don't those situations call for confrontation? It depends on what is meant by "confrontation."

Performance shortfalls need to be addressed. As discussed above, wishful thinking is a poor strategy for closing gaps in performance. In that sense, "confronting" the issue is appropriate. The difficulty is in how confrontation is typically done. A conversation that starts with an adversarial tone is rarely productive. This kind of confrontation puts the other person on the defensive. It assumes that the supervisor already has all the facts and that the staff member has nothing new to contribute in the exchange. It shuts down the flow of communication so that the employee is simply taking orders.

In contrast, it is possible to "confront" in a way that is more inviting and conversational. Doing this well starts long before the performance conversation. It begins with clarity about your expectations for the other person and their job. If you can't define what success looks like in their role, then it's impossible to have a meaningful conversation about their performance.

Think back to the story about Rusti and Jake, the new director of welcoming. Rusti was confident that she had clearly explained that Jake needed to spend time connecting with people who had visited the church, but this had not been clear to Jake. He thought that personal visits were optional and that they were a lower priority than his work on the supporting systems. In addition, by remaining silent for the first several months, Rusti had inadvertently confirmed Jake's interpretation.

Expectations aren't clear unless the other person understands them. This means that the first conversation is often one in which you realize that you need to explain the requirements of the role. Once this is clear, the person may respond positively, so that no further correction is needed. If not, you've set the stage for the right conversation about the gap between expectations and actual performance.

Actual performance is also an important concept. Those who are best at performance-redirection conversations stick to the facts and avoid guessing. It's tempting to fill in gaps in knowledge with guesses, but this will derail the conversation. In preparing for her conversation with Jake, Rusti realized that she didn't really know how many guests he had connected with. And even if he hadn't met her expectations, she had no idea why.

That leads to a final essential element in making the shift from confrontation to conversation. Becoming aware of what you don't know should lead to curiosity and questions. The right conversation most often begins with a clear statement of the performance shortfall, based only on the known facts, and then shifts to a question: "Can you help me understand why you've not met this expectation?" This is a powerful question. It acknowledges that you don't have all the facts. It moves figuratively from across-the-table confrontation to side-by-side problem-solving. It doesn't let the staff member off the hook for poor performance, but it does engage him or her in finding a solution. It allows you to enter into a real conversation.

In describing this shift, I do not want to give the impression that every conversation has a happy ending. There will be times when the final outcome is for a staff member to leave, either voluntarily or involuntarily. Those cases, however, should be few and far between. They should only occur after earlier conversations in which you have been crystal clear about the requirements of the job and have explored ways to help the person meet those expectations. If the individual continues to fall short, despite your best efforts, it's likely that the root issue is a fundamental lack of skills or a consistently bad attitude. In those cases, it's better to go through the tough termination conversation rather than letting the person linger in a job where the struggles are obvious to everyone.

In some ways, the shift from confrontation to conversation will lead to more, not less, discussions with staff members about their performance. Once you remove the perception that these interactions are always adversarial, you will see the value in offering constructive feedback. That puts you on the way to the final shift, from supervising to coaching.

From Supervising to Coaching

How do you think about your interactions with staff? Far too often, the mental model of being the "boss" focuses on being bossy—directing, correcting, monitoring, and generally being the smartest person in the room. But what if your role was to help individual staff members reach their full potential?

Of course, that is a coaching perspective, and it weaves together many of the other shifts. Rather than telling someone what to do, you're solving a problem together. Rather than giving answers, you're asking questions that help both of you develop new insights. Coaching is not an abdication of responsibility but instead is a conscious decision to release people to do their jobs. And when they struggle or fail to meet expectations, a coach helps them understand their shortfall and develop a plan to address it.

Everyone liked working for Steve. It's not that he was a pushover—far from it. Steve had high expectations for every member of the church staff, and he believed that each person could meet those expectations. Cindy had recently been hired as the worship leader for the contemporary service after the messy departure of her predecessor. Almost all of the worship volunteers had quit before Cindy arrived, so she asked Steve for funding for a paid band. This would be a quick way to turn around the situation, plus she was certain that the quality and consistency would be better with professional musicians.

Steve listened to Cindy, but he only approved enough funding for two musicians for the first three months. He then scheduled a weekly meeting to help Cindy grow in her leadership of the band. He helped her connect with some former volunteers and several new ones. Together they also worked on Cindy's organization skills so that she was able to send out songs and schedule musicians well in advance, something that the volunteers greatly appreciated. She developed confidence in her ability to work with individual band members to improve their capabilities. And she became much more adaptable in using different instruments from week to week. A year after she was hired, Cindy thanked Steve for the incredible growth that she had experienced, largely through his coaching.

Coaching is an instructive analogy in other ways as well. In sports, a good coach never loses sight of the goal. Developing individual players is a means for achieving that goal. Coaches know that players will make mistakes. They review films, not for punishment but to help players learn from their errors. At times, the coach makes the hard decision to bench a player or to move him to a different position, but this is always done for the good of the team and the player. The one thing that will earn a swift rebuke from a sports coach is a poor attitude. Giving less than 100 percent or doing something that undermines team chemistry will not be tolerated. These same practices are applicable for any ministry leader who wants to make the shift from supervising to coaching. Which of these aspects of coaching should you seek to improve?

My teen years were deeply influenced by a great coach. As a freshman in high school, the only sport in which I had a chance to excel was distance running (cross country and track). And that chance was fairly slim—I was a small kid with plenty of determination but only average athletic ability. My performance that first year was mediocre. But my coach, Gene Bosse, believed in me. My sophomore year was only slightly better. Then I had a breakout performance early in my junior year, only to suffer a series of injuries that carried over into my senior year. That February, three months before graduation and the state track meet, my prospects looked bleak. I remember a tense conversation with Coach Bosse in which I told him that trying to make a comeback seemed futile. He demonstrated a remarkable mix of compassion and resolve in that moment, and that pushed me to keep trying. When I finished second in the mile run in the state track meet that May, the place on the victory stand was just as much his as it was mine.

If you want to thrive in the second chair, be a coach. Develop your staff members to live into their full potential. Help them to tap into abilities that they may not even know they have. Don't let them off easy—it's not good for them or for your church or ministry. And when they soar, experience the joy of the victory with them.

Personal Reflection

- How do you feel about managing people? Do you enjoy it or dread it?
- Are you setting aside enough time for your staff?
- Which of the shifts described in this chapter would have the biggest impact on your staff and on your ability to thrive?
- Is there a conversation that you keep putting off, hoping that things will get better?
- Do your staff members see you as a coach? Do they know that you care about them and want them to succeed?

Discuss with Your First Chair

- Where do the two of you have significant differences in your overall philosophy for managing and developing staff? What do you need to do to get on the same page?
- Are there any specific situations that you need to discuss? Use these as a way to clarify philosophy and expectations.
- First chairs: What feedback do you have for your second chair about his or her management style? What would you like him or her to work on?
- Second chairs: Where do you need help from your first chair regarding staff management and development?

Chapter 6

Organize Selectively

A thriving second chair resists the temptation to organize everything and focuses on the places where structure is most needed and valuable.

"To organize or not to organize? That is the question." While this may be a bad take-off on Shakespeare, it's a key issue for second chair leaders.

One possible response to this question is, "Don't bother with it." After all, churches and ministries will always be somewhat chaotic. They are relatively small entities (compared to corporations) in rapidly changing environments, and they rely on volunteers. Besides, some chaos is good because it leads to creativity and innovation that can stimulate needed changes.

It's obvious that I think differently since I've identified "organize selectively" as one of the ten springs that allow a second chair to thrive. While some chaos can be a positive stimulus, too much chaos results in confusion and conflict and wasted resources. When needed systems are missing, volunteers quit, staff members work on the wrong priorities, and great ministry ideas flounder. When this happens, second chair leaders find it difficult to thrive. That's why organizing selectively is valuable.

"Organize" isn't just referring to an organization chart. While that's an important element, the organizational challenges that second chairs face are much broader. They include all of the different processes and systems of a church or ministry, from personnel policies to scheduling systems to budgeting to goal-setting and more.

In fact, this list highlights one problem. The organization challenge can feel endless. It's not hard for second chair leaders to find areas that would benefit from more structure or from clear processes. The real challenge is knowing where to focus their efforts and how to work within a system that seems to be determined to remain chaotic.

Go back for a minute to the wandering Hebrew people in the wilderness. Imagine that you're a second chair leader with Moses. With God's guidance, your leader has just led the thirsty masses to water. Moses might be able to thank God and walk away, but you're envisioning a mob scene if you don't get things organized quickly. Some sort of system is needed to make sure that everyone gets water and no one gets trampled. Which tribe goes first? Does one person go and bring water back for the family or does each person go to the spring? Should all the people get water before any of the animals?

In this moment, you will focus on organizing the access to water. Frankly, you're not going to thrive, or even rest, until you put a system in place and are sure that it's working. You may next turn your attention to organizing the campsite. Where will everyone sleep? Where should the livestock be kept? In the middle of this, if someone suggests that you need to create a system to inventory all of the gold and jewels that were plundered from the Egyptians, you may laugh at them. It might be an interesting idea, but it doesn't merit even a small footnote on your "to do" list.

This demonstrates the meaning and importance of organizing selectively. It's not done to satisfy someone's penchant for rules and order. It's done so that the group—whether that's a church or ministry or nomadic Israelites—can thrive. Because when they're thriving, the second chair leader has a chance to do the same.

Understanding Under-Organization

Churches and ministries of all different sizes and ages are chronically under-organized. Notice that I did not say *disorganized.* While the *dis-* label may be applicable in some cases, *under-* is a more accurate description of reality. Better organization is almost always needed in multiple areas. These may include an informal performance review system that needs to be formalized, a better system to forecast cash flow, or consolidation of several overlapping databases.

Under-organization occurs in churches and ministries for a variety of reasons. The biggest is that they are constantly making decisions about how to allocate limited resources, and "ministry" typically wins out over "administration." The trade-off is easy to understand. These entities exist for the purpose of doing ministry, whether it's teaching children about Jesus, creating a more inviting worship experience, or conducting job training for individuals who are unemployed. It can be difficult to make (much less win) an argument that upgrading software is more important than ministering to people. This argument applies equally to the money and the effort that may be required. As a result, the church or ministry's systems will tend to lag behind until a crisis forces a change in priorities.

The organization challenge is exacerbated in cases where the church or ministry has experienced rapid growth. The cry for resources to support ministry tends to be even more pronounced in these situations, but so does the importance of creating or upgrading systems. Another challenge is the common undercurrent that "this is not a business." When the proposed steps for better processes and systems sound as though they've been imported from the corporate arena, someone is bound to push back using this line. This argument is true in one sense. But when a ministry has a dozen (or dozens of) employees and a budget of several million dollars, applying sound organizational practices is just good stewardship.

Up to this point, the problems have all been rooted in the overall culture of the church or ministry, but there is also a personal element that second chair leaders must contend with. Actually, the personal elements come in two distinct varieties. Some second chair leaders, often those who step into the role from the world of business, are appalled when they become aware of the lack of organization. Their tendency is to try to fix everything right away. Their campaign for better organization is often met with a response of, "What's the problem?"

Landon had been moving up the ladder in a large corporation before he felt a call to ministry. After a year as an intern in the small groups ministry, he moved into a newly created position as pastor of administration. With his corporate experience, he had no shortage of ideas for ways to improve the church's operations. While some were implemented easily, others required significant changes by staff members, who quickly developed the habit of rolling their eyes when Landon had a suggestion. Landon resigned after two years, frustrated at his inability to bring about broader changes.

Highly organized second chairs like Landon are on one end of a spectrum. At the other end are the people who don't think in terms of systems or processes. This may be a function of personality or experience or both. They are often individuals who have spent much or all of their careers in ministry and may have strong pastoral or teaching gifts. They know something is amiss organizationally, but they can't clearly answer the question, "What's the solution?" because this kind of thinking doesn't come naturally.

There's actually a third personal element that comes into play, but it isn't found in the second chair—it's the first chair leader who doesn't support (at least not fully) the attempts to bring about more structure. He may agree conceptually with the benefits of less chaos, but when a second chair proposes an initiative to improve operations, the first chair is hesitant to give approval. He may decide that resources should be spent in other areas or that there will be too much resistance or that "it's not that big of a problem." Regardless of the specifics, the second chair comes away feeling hampered and frustrated.

These questions point to one of the keys for organizing selectively. If you can't articulate clearly what the problem is and why the current ways aren't working, you will never overcome the obstacles. You don't need accountant-like accuracy in this articulation, but you do need to identify the cost and impact of inadequate systems and the benefits of your proposed solution.

For example, you propose a new system to track participation in the church's small group ministry. Currently, you know how many groups exist and how many people join each group at the start of the year, but you don't know who those people are, if they've continued to participate, or if additional people joined later. The "cost" is that it's impossible to know the effectiveness of the small group ministry. If small groups are unimportant, then this cost is inconsequential. But if they are vital to your church's discipleship strategy, this lack of information *is* quite costly. At a minimum, a better system for tracking participation would provide data that would guide decisions for strengthening the small group ministry.

As you think about your church or ministry, how under-organized is it? To answer that question, it may help to think more specifically about the different dimensions where more structure may be needed.

What Are the Specific Problems?

You may wonder if this chapter is applicable for you. You may say, "We're simple and organic and *organize* is just another word for *institutionalize*." My answer is that everything that your church or ministry does has elements of organization. And if you're not intentional about how you organize, you will limit your potential.

Suppose your church "just does worship and small groups." How do you plan your worship services? Even if the pastor decides on the sermon title and Scripture passage on Friday and the worship leader then plans the service, that is still a system. What happens if parents bring young children to worship? Do you have a nursery that is divided into several classes based on their age? That also is an element of organization.

Before looking at how to organize selectively, it is helpful to identify the major categories. This can help determine where to focus limited resources. The remainder of this section touches on these categories: organization structure (org chart), goal-setting and metrics, processes related to personnel (HR), financial, ministry systems, and legal compliance.

Organization Structure

To address the problem of being under-organized, it makes sense to start with the organization chart. Creating a diagram with lines and boxes that represent individual positions and reporting relationships is a standard practice in most secular entities. While they are not uncommon in churches and ministries, I have encountered some that don't have any kind of organization chart, and far more where the chart is confusing or where it simply doesn't make sense.

Before attempting to create a "logical" organization chart, it's important to recognize some common realities that make ministry settings messier. Reporting relationships will rarely be clean. For example, the worship leader may report to the executive pastor but will still work closely with the senior pastor. Even a relatively large church and ministry will have staff members who wear multiple hats, which often connects them to multiple "bosses." In fact, when someone has a unique combination of skills, it's not unusual to write a job description that fits this specific person, even if it wouldn't make sense for anyone else. If the facilities manager is also a whiz with computers and a great cook, you take advantage of those diverse talents.

Another ministry reality is the first chair's prerogative. Their personal preferences are always an important factor in organizational design, even when those preferences don't "make sense." John was the senior pastor of a large congregation, but he continued to do an extensive amount of counseling and pastoral care. When Beth, the executive pastor, suggested that they needed to restructure the organization to reflect the church's new vision and its growth, John readily agreed. Beth presented three options, all with pastoral care reporting to her. She saw this as a way to free some of John's time for other important activities. In the end, John opted for a fourth option that cleaned up some areas but kept pastoral care reporting directly to him.

It's important for people to understand who they report to and how to resolve issues. That's why an organization chart is valuable. A wise second chair leader knows that starting from a blank sheet of paper may produce a logical structure, but acknowledging the uniqueness of the church or ministry will lead to a structure that works.

Goal-Setting and Metrics

If you want to pour your energies into an organizational issue that is both highly valuable and incredibly complex, tackle the way that your church or ministry sets goals and measures results. I know many leaders, in the first and second chair, who talk about the importance of this topic. I know very few who feel that their existing processes are working well.

Creating meaningful goals and metrics isn't easy.[1] At the heart of the challenge are three obstacles. The first is cultural resistance to accountability. When metrics are mentioned, phrases such as "too corporate" or "too harsh" are common. The second is the vagueness that often starts with the top-level vision and flows into every ministry area. Commitments to "improve the quality of the music" or "raise the spiritual temperature of the congregation" may sound nice, but they don't lead to meaningful goals.

The final obstacle is that it truly is difficult to measure the things that really matter. In most cases, the best solution is to agree on intermediate goals that indicate whether progress is being made. You can't see what is happening in the hearts of the people in your church, but you can get periodic feedback through surveys or looking at whether they are growing in their level of commitment.

Developing a process for setting goals and creating meaningful metrics is difficult. But it's far less difficult than trying to point staff members in the right direction in the absence of these systems.

Personnel Processes

A church or ministry's most valuable asset is the people who serve there, both staff and volunteers. Unfortunately, when it comes to staff, the processes for hiring, developing, evaluating, compensating, and when necessary, terminating, are often inadequate.

1. My previous book, *In Pursuit of Great AND Godly Leadership* (San Francisco: Jossey-Bass, 2012), devotes an entire chapter to this topic. Several other resources on this topic are listed in appendix C of this book.

Equally unfortunate is the fact that the broad topic of human resources can feel overwhelming for the second chair leader who is asked to get it organized. Any attempt to list all the different systems and processes related to staff could fill several pages. The list would include all of the general topics listed above with multiple subpoints such as pre-employment testing, vacation policies, progressive discipline practices, salary ranges for comparable jobs, and much more. (See appendix C for some suggested resources.)

Not only is it overwhelming, but most churches and ministries have some kind of volunteer oversight for human resources. Whether that comes through the board or a "personnel committee" (regardless of its name), there are several extra sets of eyes looking at these issues. They will often be distressed at the gaps in HR processes or offer a solution from their workplace without understanding the distinct difference between a large corporate environment and a much smaller ministry one. This only adds to the pressure that a second chair may feel.

People truly do matter. But an effective second chair leader knows that creating more structured personnel processes is a marathon, not a sprint, and that it's just one of several areas in need of organization. Some HR processes are like setting up the access to water in the desert, and others are like the inventory system for the plundered gold.

Financial

In contrast to the processes related to personnel, a church or ministry that is large enough to have multiple paid staff members generally has adequate financial systems. These include the processes and tools for receiving and recording donations, paying bills and payroll, developing budgets, and preparing financial reports.

While this area may not appear to need more organization, taking certain systems to the next level can have many benefits. For example, I am surprised at how often large ministries do not have good forecasting tools that account for seasonal swings in receipts and expenses. Without this, they may panic unnecessarily at an apparent shortfall, or they may miss warning signs of future problems. Another area that is often ripe for improvement is the interaction with donors. If a church or ministry does not proactively connect with contributors, it may be missing out on substantial funding opportunities. As second chair leaders evaluate where to focus their organizing efforts, they will do well to look below the surface of the financial systems.

Ministry Systems

Ministry systems is a catch-all term for a wide variety of formal and informal systems that are involved in running the ministry. These may relate to front-line ministry or be part of the behind-the-scene infrastructure. They may be department specific or organization wide. Examples include systems and processes for:

- planning worship services,
- assimilating new members,
- recruiting and training volunteers,
- placing people in small groups,
- assigning mentors to kids in an after-school tutoring program,
- calendaring events and scheduling rooms,
- communicating important news (internally and externally),
- tracking the services provided to a client,
- screening and selecting people to serve in leadership roles.

Everything that a church or ministry does has supporting systems. The question isn't whether the systems exist but how well they are working and which ones deserve attention.

Legal Compliance

The final category, legal compliance, can be the most complicated. It cuts across some of the earlier categories, especially personnel, but it deserves separate mention. Churches and ministries are surrounded by a vast minefield of local, state, and federal laws and regulations. They relate to virtually every aspect of employment—discrimination, exempt versus nonexempt, benefits, and on-the-job injuries to name a few. Other laws affect governance, financial management, day care, food services, counseling, and more. Some have limited consequence while others carry the possibility of criminal charges, large fines, or loss of tax exempt status. I don't know of any church or ministry leader who sets out to intentionally violate these laws. But most would say in private that they doubt they are in full compliance with every regulation.

When I served as an executive pastor, I struck a deal with our business manager. She regularly attended seminars in order to keep up with the various regulations. After these seminars, she would often present me with a list of things that we needed to change in order to be in full compliance. After several of these meetings, we both began to feel overwhelmed. Addressing all of the issues simultaneously was not only impossible but would detract from our ministries. So I asked her to prioritize the list, with the issues that had the greatest potential consequences for the church at the top. My side of the deal was to provide the resources and run interference so that we could address these top priorities.

Processes for legal compliance may never seem to be high priority—until you suffer the consequences of noncompliance. That's why this category can't be ignored as you think about how to organize selectively.

Now that you have looked over this list and have begun to see the breadth of processes and systems that are involved, how under-organized is your church or ministry? More importantly, where should you focus? After all, the chapter title isn't "Organize Everything." If you try to do that, you can't possibly thrive. The title is "Organize Selectively." What does that look like in your context?

The Key Qualifier—*Selective*

It is clear that a second chair leader will never run out of opportunities for filling organizational gaps in a church or ministry. But knowing that a gap exists doesn't mean that it needs to be addressed. Taking an inventory of plundered gold may never become a priority.

Organizing selectively means focusing on the structures, processes, and systems that will have the greatest impact on the church or ministry. As you look at all the different areas that could be organized better, what systems and processes are most needed to accomplish the mission? Which will produce the greatest benefit relative to the cost?

In some cases, these questions will be answered as you "think strategically" (see chapter 4) and develop plans for the coming year. A nonprofit may have relied heavily on one supporter, so the leadership team determines that expanding the base of donors is a key priority. Their selective organization involves: (a) combining multiple databases into one to facilitate better communication with donors, (b) systematically collecting stories of ministry success to be used in future communications, and (c) developing a process to identify people who should receive special attention (e.g., new donors to thank, potential large contributors to build relationships with).

In other cases, organizational improvement ideas don't emerge from the planning process because the needs are less obvious. I rarely hear a leader say that investing in better personnel practices is a top priority. But that doesn't mean that these less visible systems are unimportant. It just means that the planning process is focused on ministry and assumes that the supporting systems will be adequate. Unfortunately, this is a bad assumption.

As you can see, the steps you should take to organize selectively may lead in a number of directions. After all, every church or ministry is unique. Based on my experience with a variety of churches, the four most important principles are: put people first, translate vision into goals, don't reinvent the wheel, and remember that it's not a business.

Put People First

Getting the right people in the right seats on the bus is a key principle from Jim Collins's *Good to Great*.[2] Every ministry leader wants to have the right people, but few establish the right processes to insure this outcome. While the specific ideas that follow focus on people who are in paid positions, the importance of getting the right people on the bus is just as true for those in volunteer leadership roles.

How much time do you invest in the selection process for the people who will be serving with you and helping to lead your church or ministry? Plenty of people may think that they are "right," so creating an effective process for selection is critical. It shouldn't be an afterthought.

You can't find the right people if you don't know what you're looking for. Time must be spent to develop a meaningful job description. Similarly, it takes time to find great people who will meet your requirements and fit your church or ministry. The best processes search extensively and always consider multiple candidates for the job. They engage in multiple rounds of screening and interviews to thoroughly evaluate whether the person has the skills that are needed and how they will fit the culture. If the basis for a hiring decision is "we couldn't

2. Jim Collins, *Good to Great: Why Some Companies Make the Leap... and Others Don't* (New York: HarperCollins, 2001), 41.

find anyone else" or "he seemed like a nice guy," it's unlikely that you've found the right person.

The time required to hire the right people is a significant investment. To protect that investment, you need to spend the time to onboard them well. The prevailing model in many ministries is "plug-and-play," which implicitly assumes that onboarding isn't needed if you hire good people. But even an experienced person needs more help in those first few months than can be found in a two-day orientation or a personnel manual. They need someone who will help them understand the countless unwritten rules for "how we do things." They will be much more effective if they're aware of the hidden land mines. And they need to know what is expected of them.

Everyone, regardless of role or tenure, needs to know how success is defined and whether they are meeting that standard. Putting people first means creating an evaluation process that gives meaningful feedback to every staff member. The best processes are part of a broader coaching philosophy (discussed in the previous chapter). They are fair and consistent. They reinforce the behavior that is most important for the ministry's culture and they connect clearly to the overall vision.

Translate Vision into Goals

The book of Judges ends with the haunting phrase, "Everyone did what was right in his own eyes" (Judg 21:25 ESV). Could those words be used to describe your church or ministry? Not that individual leaders are doing things that are wrong or evil, but they may be working independently of each other with little regard for the church or ministry's overall direction.

While it might be tempting to blame rogue staff members for this behavior, it is likely that one of the culprits is a process problem. If you do not have a meaningful way to translate the overall vision into ministry-specific goals, then you're giving each person the freedom to do whatever seems right in their own eyes. In contrast, an effective process is a bridge that uses strategic thinking (see chapter 4) to create individual ministry plans and to promote overall alignment.

One church's next priority was to hire a youth director to extend the booming children's ministry. The leadership team wanted the youth to have a strong discipleship orientation via small groups, just like the adults. David, the church's business manager, recruited a small team of volunteers to spearhead this effort. After writing a thorough job description, they began the hiring process. They rejected a number of candidates who had great credentials but didn't fit their philosophy or culture and were thrilled when the search led to Kara.

David worked closely with Kara to help her get up to speed and develop specific goals. They agreed that the most important objectives in her first year were to build a strong team of small group leaders and to establish a sustainable model for how these groups would function. It wasn't long before Kara was being pressured by some parents to hold several attractional events and to spend more time hanging out with the youth. Fortunately, she understood her priorities and knew that she had David's support. While growth was slow at first, the strong foundation that they built led to a vibrant program for many years afterward.

The best processes for setting goals are directly related to the church or ministry's overall vision. These processes are both top down and bottom up—the former because individual plans and goals relate directly to the vision and the latter because they are developed by the people who will be responsible for doing the work. This typically requires an iterative process with a second chair who is willing to challenge the plans and goals that are proposed by staff members. These processes also tie in to the evaluation system as discussed in the previous section. When a staff member can articulate how her goals support the vision and knows that she will be evaluated accordingly, a powerful virtuous cycle is created.

Don't Reinvent the Wheel

The previous two sections relate to specific kinds of processes, while this one and the next focus on the mind-sets that will help second chairs be more effective as they organize selectively. The first is simple: if you want to accelerate your organizational efforts, take advantage of the work that others have done already.

Many resources are available for second chair leaders who are willing to look and ask. A great deal of information can be found online in free or inexpensive articles and webinars. Just type the topic of interest into your favorite search engine, and you may be surprised at how much you will discover. In addition to information, you can find tools and content that can be customized to fit your needs, including policies, personnel manuals, job descriptions, evaluation forms, and more. Sources include associations, denominational bodies, large churches, and vendors. I've listed a few general sources in appendix C.

Ministry colleagues at other churches are another great source of ideas and tools. Because they're not in competition, many will readily share processes that they've developed (or found) or spend a few hours to discuss how they're addressing a particular need. The solution to your problem may be as easy as sending a few emails or making a few calls.

Technology is another important resource to avoid reinventing the wheel. Someone within the staff should be a champion for leveraging technology, and the company that provides your primary database software should be a key ally in your efforts to organize selectively and effectively. As you're exploring new or improved processes, particularly related to the "ministry systems" mentioned earlier in this chapter, ask how to get the most benefit from technology.

As you consider these resources, keep in mind that you're looking for a functional solution, not a perfect one. You could spend hours creating the ideal process or system, but if something off-the-shelf is good enough, the time that you save is usually better spent elsewhere.

Remember It's Not a Business

Have you ever had an organizational improvement idea rejected with the phrase "It's not a business"? While I believe that this catchphrase is used too often, it does have merit. The processes and structures that have been built for large, for-profit environments typically fit a church or ministry about as well as a mom's high-heeled shoes fit the feet of her eight-year-old daughter. The girl may be able to walk in the shoes, but she will be clumsy and prone to tripping. Ideas from business may be helpful in ministry settings, but they need to be adapted, not adopted.

Jessica had a successful career in the publishing business before becoming the first associate director at her growing compassion ministry. As often happens, the ministry's organization had not kept pace with the expansion. One of her first priorities was to implement their first system for performance reviews. She took the multi-page form used in her former company, modified it slightly, and rolled it out. The result was confusion and frustration. The staff simply had no idea how to use this new process effectively. Six months later, she implemented a new one-page form, this time with input from staff and training in how it was to be used. The difference in organizational impact and the staff's receptivity was dramatic.

If you keep hearing "it's not a business," especially if you've entered the second chair from the marketplace, you may need to shift your mind-set. Even though you're bringing great experience and ideas to the table, it's possible that you need to be more sensitive to your context and to work harder to adapt the new systems accordingly.

A final mind-set that encompasses this entire chapter is to *think like a gardener*. When talking about processes and systems, second chair leaders often express a desire for the church or ministry to be a "well-oiled machine." A better analogy is to strive to have a well-watered garden. (I'm indebted to Kyle Nabors, executive pastor of Kensington Church, for this concept.) The machine image suggests that every part needs to be in perfect working order. If the radiator hose for your car has a leak, you won't go very far. One small piece out of place can cause the entire machine to stop running.

A garden, on the other hand, is never perfect. There is always work to be done. There are always weeds to be pulled and plants to be pruned or staked. But these imperfections don't mean that the garden won't be productive. Even if you get behind on your weeding or overwater by a little, you can still have a great harvest.

When it comes to organizing selectively, that's really what every second chair leader wants. If they are experiencing a great harvest—if the systems are working well enough that the ministry is producing the desired, God-honoring results—then no one should worry about a few weedy-looking processes. That's the kind of gardening that allows a second chair leader to thrive.

Personal Reflection

- As you review the different categories of systems and processes listed in this chapter, how would you rate your church or ministry?
- Where is improvement most needed? What's the basis for your answer?
- Do you have clear goals for the church or ministry overall and for individual departments?
- Do you tend to push too hard to use processes from business? Or are you too resistant to ideas from business?

Discuss with Your First Chair

- Are you both on the same page regarding the overall importance of processes and systems? Where are the greatest specific needs?
- How could changes in processes or systems improve ministry effectiveness?
- Second chairs: What support do you need from your first chair in this area?

Chapter 7

Navigate Governance Nuances

Thriving second chair leaders don't overstep their boundaries but navigate the delicate dance with boards and committees in ways that advance the mission, support the first chair, and maintain unity.

"Would you like me to cover the finance committee meeting tomorrow night so that you can go home and be with your family?"

From John's perspective, it was a simple and innocent question that made perfect sense. He had been in a second chair role at the nonprofit agency for over a year. From the beginning, he and Becky (the first chair) had talked about dividing responsibilities for committee meetings so that they could each have less evening commitments. John had a business background and had attended all of the finance meetings over the past year. This particular meeting was a midyear review and the agenda was routine.

So John was surprised at Becky's hesitation and the brief scowl that he saw on her face. He wondered to himself, *Did I do something wrong?*

It's Just Common Sense, Right?

Governance boards and committees are part of the leadership equation in any church or ministry. They may have a variety of names—board, elders, deacons, session, vestry, church council. Size and role may vary as well. Most organizations have several important committees (such as finance and personnel) in addition to the top-level governing body. Some have a large number of committees, each requiring a degree of staff interaction. Regardless of names and structures, boards and committees can serve a valuable purpose.

This value comes with a cost. The interactions with each of these groups requires time and energy. At least one senior-level person from the staff is usually involved in preparing for and participating in each meeting and in the conversations with committee members that may be needed between meetings. So it does seem like common sense to use this time efficiently by dividing responsibilities between leaders. The presence of both first and second chair leaders may be appropriate at key meetings, but not the run-of-the-mill ones. In fact, the second chair often has the detailed information and the temperament that is needed for the interaction with many of these bodies.

So if this kind of division is so logical, why do many second chairs experience a reaction like the one John received? The answer may be as simple (and frustrating) as an insecure first chair. Perhaps she is worried about what will be said when she's not in the room or that her absence will trigger criticism that she's not doing her job. Perhaps the first chair leader doesn't have confidence in the second chair's ability to go solo in the meeting.

While all of these may be true, two other factors often come into play. The first chair leader may have relevant information that the second chair doesn't know. You would hope that this wouldn't happen, especially in a high trust environment, but it often does. Becky may know that the finance chair is anxious about a dip in donations. Or she may have heard that one of the committee members is planning to challenge the staff's request to spend designated funds for a new marketing initiative.

The second factor is at the heart of the challenge with governance bodies and committees. No matter how long a first and second chair have worked together or how much effort they put into staying on the same page, minor differences between them are inevitable. In the context of these powerful and influential decision-making groups, those small gaps can quickly turn into large and harmful divisions.

Mind the Gap

If you've ever been to London and taken the Underground (subway), you're undoubtedly familiar with the expression "Mind the gap." It's their way of saying to be careful of the small space between the platform and the car as you're getting on and off the subway. Why is this such a big deal? After all, the gap is quite small. It's hard to imagine accidents being a frequent occurrence. It may just be a British tradition. But perhaps it's because the consequences of not minding the gap are huge. A person who isn't paying attention could wedge his foot in this space, which would result in a serious injury when the subway starts to move.

In your normal duties as a second chair, small gaps between you and the first chair are not a major concern. He may think that it's time to launch a new mission partnership and you think that the staff needs a couple more months to make sure that the current one is working well. She sees one of the young staff members as a rising star who is ready for more responsibility. You also see a rising star, but think that more seasoning is needed in the current role. These are not the kinds of issues that undermine trust or cause severe conflict between first and second chairs.

But these small gaps can become serious if they are exposed in a board or committee meeting. Go back to Becky and John's meeting with the finance committee and the new marketing initiative that she is proposing. John and Becky agreed on the need for more marketing. They worked together closely in developing the recommendation, and they saw eye-to-eye on most of the key points. John only had two concerns. He thought that a slightly larger budget would greatly increase the effectiveness of the marketing efforts, and he wanted to emphasize social media more. Becky listened to John's input, but she was concerned about stretching too far financially, so the final proposal didn't go as far as John wanted. Nevertheless, he was pleased that they were trying to take a step forward.

Fast-forward and imagine the meeting. If one of the finance committee members asks John for his thoughts on the marketing proposal, what will he say? If he mentions that the budget should be bigger, the once-small gap between him and Becky can suddenly become much larger. If Becky is in the meeting, all eyes will turn to her. How will she respond? Will she and John have to work through their differences in front of the committee? If she is not in the meeting, it is possible that the committee will approve a revised initiative based on John's input or will table the decision until a future meeting when Becky is present. But far more important than the marketing decision is the impact that this has on Becky and John's relationship and the perception of the committee members.

With healthy leadership teams and high trust levels, honest disagreements are welcomed in meetings. But no one, regardless of tenure or trust, wants a board or key committee to perceive a leadership schism. John may think that it's just a small gap and that he was simply expressing his opinion. Becky may have a completely different perception. She may use words such as "embarrassed" to describe her feelings, or "undermining" to label John's actions, or "disaster" to summarize the meeting.

Is this an overreaction by Becky (and any other first chair who responds in a similar manner)? Not as much as you might think. Virtually anyone who sits in the first chair has memories of opposition from a board or key committee. Those memories may be from a past church or ministry or the current one, or may even be the horror stories told by a colleague. Regardless of the details, every first chair leader knows that small gaps can cause big headaches if they become public. Three of the problematic ways that lay leaders may respond to perceived first-second chair gaps are:

- *Losing confidence in the first chair.* The conversation about a specific topic may reveal that the first chair leader has not done a good job of thinking through the details. Even though this is just one topic, the board or committee may begin to wonder if this is representative of a broader pattern or a leadership deficiency.

- *Meddling in operational details.* Board and committee members rarely receive appropriate training or instruction on their roles, so they are unclear about where their responsibilities end and staff responsibilities begin. In effective churches and ministries, boards and committees stay at the higher levels of strategy and policy. When gaps appear, however, they are much more likely to dive into the operational details.

- *Taking sides.* A gap between first and second chairs creates an opportunity for lay leaders to take sides. It's unpleasant if they do so in the meeting, but it can be disastrous if this occurs outside of the meeting. What may start as a casual one-on-one conversation over coffee the next week can turn into an inquiry into the (perceived) shortcomings of the first chair.

These may be some of the thoughts that run through Becky's mind in the flash of a second when John offers to cover the finance committee meeting. It's not that she thinks that John is disloyal. It's just that she's aware of the damage that can be done by small gaps.

In truth, gaps can appear even if first and second chair are both in the meeting and the second chair never opens his mouth. A furrowed brow or uncomfortable body language may signal to a board member that a gap exists.

Lisa had been executive pastor at her church for two years when the senior pastor surprisingly announced that he was leaving to take a denominational position. Attendance had been flat for almost a decade, and during the interim period, the church had to dip into its financial reserves to cover a small deficit. Lisa provided capable leadership during this time, meeting with all the key committees and holding the line on spending, and she was thrilled when Will arrived as the new senior pastor. Within six months, Will had outlined a plan for several turnaround initiatives and had scheduled a meeting with the personnel committee to request approval for two new full-time positions.

Lisa and Will had a lengthy discussion before the meeting. She was supportive of all three initiatives but was concerned about the church's ability to fund them. She suggested that they stage the initiatives, starting one in the current year with the others to follow. Doing so would only require one new part-time staff member initially. Will had listened respectfully to Lisa, but closed the meeting by saying, "This church has enormous untapped resources. People give to support a bold vision. We can't wait."

During the committee meeting the next week, one of the most financially conservative members asked Lisa for her opinion about the proposal. Lisa expressed support, even repeating Will's phrase that people would give to a bold vision. But to those who knew Lisa well, something was missing in her tone and facial expressions that indicated a lack of enthusiasm for this idea. The next day, the committee member e-mailed Lisa to ask if they could meet sometime in the next week.

The truth is that lay leaders can lose confidence or meddle or take sides, even if a second chair leader never attends a meeting and even if the only gap is in their imagination. This is the messiness of leadership in a church or ministry. The question for second chair leaders who want to thrive is how they can interact with boards and committees in positive ways that mind the gaps and help the organization achieve its God-given potential.

Doing the Heavy Lifting

At this point, you may be thinking that it's best to just lay low and not have any interaction with committees and governance bodies. While this area can be a minefield to navigate, you can't escape the common-sense logic that argues for your involvement. Your first chair's time, as well as your own, is a precious resource for the organization, and it should be managed effectively. You also want to use your leadership gifts, and it's hard to imagine using those gifts in a second chair role apart from involvement with the key lay leadership teams.

But the main reason that second chairs need to interact with governance bodies and committees goes far beyond the actual meetings. These are the groups that will make (or at least be involved in) the key strategic decisions for the church or ministry, and heavy lifting must be done in order to make wise decisions. Think of all the work that goes into preparing the annual budget or creating a new organizational structure or developing the annual goals.

Of course, the first chair could do the majority of this heavy lifting, but this is not likely to be the best use of his time and may not play to his strengths. Similarly, the first chair could handle all the interactions with the board and committees but rely on staff to do the majority of the preparatory work. In most cases, however, this option is not any better. Unless the first chair has a great ability to absorb the details, the board and committee members will quickly grow frustrated at the lack of specific answers to their questions.

That's where you come in! The second chair is frequently expected to be the person who meets this need. Whether you actually do the heavy lifting or oversee staff members who handle different tasks, you are positioned to see the big picture and understand the details. As such, your contribution to the church or ministry's decision-making is invaluable. So the question isn't whether to be involved, but how.

Lifting weights isn't inherently dangerous, but anyone who wants to lift should follow some basic precautions in order to stay safe. In the same way, the remainder of this chapter explores some simple precautions that will help you do the heavy lifting for working effectively with governance and leadership groups.

Before the Meeting

Everyone knows about the "meeting after the meeting" that can occur in the parking lot when a subset of a committee rehashes the decisions that were just made. This is usually an unhealthy event. But for first and second chair leaders, a pre-meeting can be one of the most important ways to mind the gap.

The concept is simple—the pre-meeting is a prep meeting. It's an opportunity to review the agenda and to make sure that first and second chair are on the same page regarding key points and roles in the meeting. They can discuss any areas where tension is anticipated and talk about how this should be handled. They can communicate information that the other may not know. And they should certainly discuss any points where they have different perspectives.

This kind of pre-meeting is just as valuable for committee meetings that the first chair is not going to attend. The pre-meeting gives the first chair the chance to share any messages that she wants the second chair to convey to the committee. It's also an opportunity to talk about boundaries and contingencies for the meeting. How much authority does the second chair have in the first chair's absence? What should the second chair do if the meeting goes in an unexpected, negative direction?

I'm not suggesting that the entire meeting can be scripted or that differing opinions during the meeting are to be squelched. I am saying that it's important to try to avoid embarrassing moments (or worse) where it is clear that the first and second chair leaders are not on the same page. This requires setting aside the time for another meeting, but the potential value of having a pre-meeting can far exceed the cost. With long-term partnerships, the pre-meeting may eventually become unnecessary, but don't be too quick to eliminate this step.

In the Meeting

Preparing for these key meetings is important, but it's impossible to anticipate every twist and turn that might take place. Consider these scenarios:

- During the statistical review in the quarterly board meeting, a member interrupts you and pointedly asks, "Why do you think that we've been trending down for the past eighteen months?"

- The personnel committee is discussing a proposal to add a mission director to the staff, when one of the members interjects serious concerns about the performance of the youth director.

- After several months of planning, the board is having its final meeting to approve a capital campaign. One member, who is also expected to be a major contributor, expresses concerns out of left field that the timing isn't right for the campaign.

These are just three examples out of an almost endless range of possibilities. You can undoubtedly fill in the blank with your own stories. No matter how much you prepare, you cannot predict or control the behavior of the others in the room.

In your second chair role, you might think that the solution is to keep your mouth shut in these cases. But that may leave the first chair out on a limb. It may not be possible if a comment or question is directed to you, or if the first chair is not present.

Regardless of whether the first chair is in the meeting, two guidelines can help prevent the creation of an unintended gap: disagree behind closed doors and don't rush to decide. Just as in the earlier example with Becky and John, you and your first chair will inevitably have matters where you are not in complete agreement. In general, these discussions should take place before the meeting, behind closed doors. Once the meeting starts, you need to be of one accord. You need to use "we" language to communicate that you are together.

One exception to this guideline is if the two of you have explicitly agreed to share both perspectives with the board or committee so that they can make the final decision. Becky and John could decide to share both ideas on the marketing campaign in order to seek the board's input, especially if some board members have expertise in this area. This should only be done in a spirit of genuinely seeking broader counsel, not as a tie-breaker for an argument. Even in the case of seeking counsel, second chairs should air their differences with the utmost respect.

The second guideline—don't rush to decide—is particularly relevant when a board or committee member throws an unexpected curve. In the moment, you may feel that you need to give an immediate response. When the question is raised about the youth director's performance, it may seem as though you have to deal with it. But you have other options. You can finish the discussion about the mission director position and put the youth director discussion on the agenda for the next meeting. Or you can explore the committee member's concerns and then ask for time to investigate. Delaying a decision is often a wise choice, and it gives you the opportunity to get on the same page with your first chair.

In most churches and ministries, the senior pastor (or first chair) will participate in the key meetings, including those with the governing body and certain committee meetings (e.g., budget presentation and approval with the finance committee). In cases where you are both present in the meeting, you can take several other practical steps:

- *Keep a line of sight.* Where you sit in a meeting can make all the difference in the world. Choose a place where you have an easy and direct line of sight to your first chair. When surprises arise, look for clues on how to respond.

- *Look for signals.* If you have a line of sight, you can see your first chair's slight shake or nod of the head that lets you know whether you should speak. A distant look or checking a cell phone indicates disengagement. An intense stare or an anxious expression can tell you that this is a touchy issue.

- *Don't speak until it's your turn.* You may have relevant information, but that doesn't mean you should speak immediately. Through the relationship you've built with your first chair, and any specific pre-meeting guidance, you should know when it will be appropriate to speak and when you should stay quiet.

- *Manage your own body language.* It's not easy to control body language, but you should be aware of how you are reacting during a meeting. A scowl or looking away can sometimes communicate more than your spoken words.

Your words and actions in these meetings will have a direct impact on how well you thrive, but they are not the only factor to consider.

After the Meeting

A simple but often overlooked step is to debrief after meetings, especially when an important issue has been discussed or a surprising twist has occurred. This quick conversation between first and second chair can have a lasting impact.

If the first chair did not participate in the meeting, it is essential to bring him up to speed. The second chair needs to communicate any major decisions, controversies, or deviations from plans that occurred. A first chair leader who gets blindsided after a committee meeting, due to lack of communication from the second chair, will be reluctant to give this much responsibility to the second chair in the future.

Even when first and second chairs both attend a meeting, the follow-up conversation is valuable. It's a chance for the second chair to ask if she should have done anything differently or if she has unintentionally offended the first chair. If so, she can promptly apologize and correct the misunderstanding. This conversation is also the time to agree on any next steps that need to be taken and who will do so.

Nathan had been hired to fill the second chair for his regional denominational body. In addition to general leadership responsibilities, he was expected to manage the renovation of a building that would become their new office. During a meeting of the ad hoc committee that was overseeing this major project, one of the members asked Nathan if he felt confident about the contractor's bid. Nathan answered that it was a fixed-price contract that he had reviewed carefully and that he was confident everything was in order.

After the meeting, Nathan sat down with his boss, Darren. Darren pointed out that Nathan's answer in the meeting came across as defensive and left little room for additional questions. The committee member who had asked the questions had experience in construction and could have provided a valuable second set of eyes on the contract. Nathan apologized to Darren and agreed to reach out to the committee member to invite him to look over the bid.

A debrief meeting may be a five-minute conversation at the coffee bar, or it may be much more extensive. But either way, it's far better than allowing lessons to go unlearned or misunderstandings to go uncorrected.

Beyond the Meeting

Meetings with the board and other key committees are an important aspect of leading any church or ministry. But just as important are the informal interactions outside of those meetings. I'm not talking about a passing greeting on a Sunday morning but rather the one-on-one conversations where much of the heavy lifting is done before and after the formal gatherings. It's the discussion with the finance chair about the terms of the new loan agreement. It's visiting over coffee with a board member who is frustrated that the new strategy isn't missional enough.

Someone needs to carry this load. Sometimes it is obvious that the "someone" should be the first chair, such as meeting with the board chair or dealing with an issue that no one else can handle. Sometimes it is obvious that the second chair is the right person, generally in cases where he has the specific knowledge or expertise that is needed. And in many cases, the "someone" could be either the first or a second chair leader.

So which should it be? Ideally, the decision will be based on how to best add value and advance the church or ministry toward its mission. If the first chair has other priorities for how to spend his time and the second chair can handle most of these interactions, then that should be the determining factor. They might divide their responsibilities by committees—the senior pastor relates to the elders and the personnel committee, and the executive pastor relates to the finance and property/facility committees. They might decide on an ad hoc basis.

Just as these informal interactions are a vital part of leadership, they are also a place where small gaps (or even nonexistent ones) can grow quickly. The executive pastor schedules a meeting with the member of the personnel committee who had concerns about the youth director. The purpose of the meeting is clear—the executive pastor wants to hear the concerns, correct any misperceptions, and decide on next steps before the committee's next meeting. But as they finish talking about the youth director, the committee member says that his real concern is that the senior pastor is too soft in dealing with performance problems. Instantly, the second chair is placed in a dangerous and vulnerable position.

If you serve in the second chair long enough, you will encounter this kind of situation. You can't prevent it. But you can be aware that divisive moments are always possible, and that even a superficial response can be blown out of proportion. Awareness should help you be prepared. Not that you can plan your answer, but you can remember the danger of saying anything that could be divisive or taken out of context in a negative way. The appropriate response will be dictated by the context, but it is often advisable to end the conversation rather than get into a debate, ask the committee member to talk to the senior pastor directly, and give the first chair a heads-up.

Putting It into Practice

My church experienced a successful pastoral transition during my time as executive pastor. Our long-tenured, beloved senior pastor was succeeded by an equally beloved but much younger associate. Our new senior pastor, Roger, recognized that our bylaws were woefully outdated. Bylaws are generally something you don't pay attention to until you really need them, and then it becomes crucial to have ones that are well written. While we didn't anticipate any problems post-transition, we didn't want to be caught unprepared.

Few first chair leaders want to spend their time working on a major revision of the bylaws. At the same time, any first chair leader will be concerned about the impact of these changes. Both were true for Roger, so a former deacon chair and I were tasked with co-leading an ad hoc team on this project. As we sorted through a number of different questions and options, I knew the issues that would be of greatest interest to Roger and kept him appropriately informed. I also saved him from dealing with the many other details that didn't concern him. At one point, I paused the process so that I could get his input on an issue where I was unsure of his opinion. At another point, I advocated strongly for something that mattered deeply to him.

While we made a number of changes, the biggest was a shift in the church's governance structure. This is not the kind of change that is taken lightly by lay leadership or a senior pastor. We knew that the full support of the ad hoc team would be needed to gain church approval. Even though navigating toward an effective and acceptable solution felt like a balancing act at times, the end result was widely supported and has continued to serve the church well. And just as importantly, the process didn't become a burden to the senior pastor.

This story highlights two final principles about the ways that second chair leaders should work with boards and committees. While no one can be a mind-reader, the most effective second chairs have a tremendous ability to anticipate the priorities and reactions of their first chairs. The more they grow toward partnership (chapter 1), the more proficient they become in this ability. These second chairs also keep the end in mind at all times. They may deal with many details in their work with leadership teams and they will experience moments of tension, but they don't let this distract them from the team's ultimate purpose.

This chapter has had a number of warnings about things that could go wrong for second chair leaders as they work with governance bodies and committees. So let me close by encouraging you to not walk away from the table. In the second chair, you have an opportunity to work with lay leadership groups to advance the mission, support your first chair, and maintain unity. That's an opportunity that is worth taking some risks to pursue.

Personal Reflection

- What role would you like to play with the governance body and other committees? What role do you need to play? (Your answers to these questions may not be the same.)
- Is there any tension between you and your first chair related to the board and/or committees? If so, do you know why?
- Which of the recommended steps will be most helpful for you?

Discuss with Your First Chair

- Discuss whether either of you has any concerns about interactions with the board or committees.
- Clarify expectations about each of your responsibilities with the board and various committees.
- Second chairs: Ask your first chair how you can best support him or her in working with the board and committees.
- First chairs: If your second chair will handle some of these responsibilities on his or her own, explain your expectations, including what kind of communication and information you need.
- Talk about the value of pre- and post-meetings, and decide if this should become a standard practice.

Chapter 8

Seek Lasting Rewards

Second chairs who thrive don't depend on affirmation from their first chair, other leaders, or tangible accomplishments because their identity is anchored in Christ.

"I have labored to no purpose. I have spent my strength in vain and for nothing." I don't know how many times I've heard words like this from a second chair leader who is in the midst of a season of discouragement.

Bill was a talented and versatile leader. He had successfully led youth and music ministries in several different churches before stepping into an executive pastor role. When Bill and I met, he had been in the second chair for two years, and he was struggling. Not that the church was struggling—all of the indicators were positive. But Bill was accustomed to having something tangible to show for his work—numerical and spiritual growth of the students or high points in the church calendar when music was the central element. "How do I know if I'm succeeding?" was the question that hung over our conversation.

Bill is not alone. Things may be going well in the church, but the second chair doesn't feel that his contributions are recognized or valued. Or the ministry may be suffering through a difficult period that is forcing the leadership team to rethink the mission or even its future existence. In these and many other scenarios, a second chair leader may think, *What's the point? I have spent my strength in vain and for nothing.*

That is why it is important to complete the quote: "Yet what is due me is in the Lord's hand, and my reward is with my God." These words—from Isaiah

49:4—have become one of my most important life verses. If you want to thrive in the second chair, you should hide these words in your heart as well.

Laboring to No Purpose?

Doesn't every job have ups and downs, good seasons and difficult ones? Of course. Are these any different for a second chair leader than for others in ministry? I believe that they are different because the "ups" are often not as high, and the "downs" can be particularly intense.

Go back to Bill. It's only human to want to see the fruit of one's efforts. But what is that fruit when you're in the second chair? If the church or ministry is thriving, people will point to one or more specific elements as being responsible. "It's our children's/youth/small group/missions/worship ministry that makes this such a vibrant church." They may point to the preaching of the senior pastor or the charismatic leadership of a homeless agency's first chair. Whatever they highlight is connected to a person (usually a staff member, occasionally a volunteer) who has direct responsibility for making it happen. And that person isn't the second chair.

At times a second chair leader has a more direct role for one aspect of the church or ministry. It may be an area that doesn't have a dedicated staff member or a special initiative like a capital campaign or an all-church, off-campus anniversary worship service. But these hands-on duties tend to be a relatively small portion of the job.

Even when the second chair has a direct responsibility, it may go unnoticed. That's because the public portion of the task may be handled by the first chair leader. A growing church begins to wonder if God might be leading them to become multisite. The senior pastor appoints a task force to pray about this decision and to explore the many different questions that need to be addressed, and he asks the executive pastor to lead the group. After three months of hard work, the recommendation to add a satellite campus is going to be made to the church council and then to the congregation.

Who will present the recommendation? In many cases, it will be the senior pastor. Sure, the executive pastor will be in the meeting and may discuss some of the details or answer questions. But the senior pastor will have much of the spotlight. Is this inappropriate? Am I describing an ego-driven or insecure senior pastor? Perhaps. But it could simply be a senior pastor who knows that the church won't approve this major decision unless he plays a visible role in supporting it.

Thriving in the second chair requires coming to grips with these realities. Staff members who work for you will get credit when their individual ministries are soaring. No one will know about the long meetings you had with those staff members to help them develop the ideas that led to this success. Church members will be thrilled with the great results from a church-wide initiative, but they won't know that you spent hours coordinating the efforts of multiple staff members and volunteers in order to produce the final results. And when the first chair leader announces a new strategic emphasis—such as the launch of a satellite campus—few people will realize the role that you played in getting to this point.

These are the challenges when things are going well, and it's certainly not any better when a church or ministry is struggling. Those who serve in second chair roles are leaders who see the big picture, so they feel the weight of poor results almost as much as the person in the first chair. In difficult seasons, second chair leaders will experience the stress of trying to develop plans that will lead to a much-needed turnaround. They will agonize over the possibility of layoffs. They will feel responsible for the mistakes or performance shortfalls of others that led to this point. They may even be blamed (by the first chair or key leaders) for these implementation failures.

Fulfillment for second chair leaders is also directly linked to their relationship with the first chair. Things can be going great for the church, but if this key relationship is strained, the second chair may find herself on the margin. When the ministry is not doing well, relational stress may lead to unjustified blame for the second chair. In contrast, when the relationship is healthy, good seasons feel like shared victories and times of struggle are not borne alone.

Outside of the church or ministry, second chair leaders will find few people who understand and recognize what they do. Ministry colleagues and denominational leaders often don't "get it." When someone refers to you as "just an associate," it stings. It suggests that you don't have a significant leadership role and that your contributions are marginal.

It also stings when you are criticized unfairly or attacked by people within the church or ministry. It seems that every second chair has at least one scar caused by someone who didn't agree with a leadership decision or just didn't like them personally. Our settings are supposed to be places where Christ-like behavior is the norm, but they're often just the opposite. At times, it's enough to make anyone feel as though they are laboring to no purpose.

I hope you work for a great first chair who publicly acknowledges your work and privately appreciates the great value that you bring to the church or ministry.

I hope that you have others inside and outside the ministry who recognize your contributions. I hope that your church or ministry is continually taking new ground for the Kingdom. If so, it may be easy for you to experience deep fulfillment in your work. For those seasons and situations when this is not true, the rest of this chapter is for you.

Finding Fulfillment

Let's assume that you are not working for a first chair leader who easily gives credit and encouragement and that you're not surrounded by people who affirm the value of your contributions. Does that mean you just need to find another spring that will quench your thirst for thriving? While it may be more difficult to thrive in this environment, it's not impossible.

I had been in the second chair role for about four years, and had not had a meaningful performance review since my one-year anniversary. (The annual reviews since then had been less than five minutes long with the message being, "Keep up the good work.") I asked our senior pastor if we could schedule a time for a more complete review. In response, I got a couple of extra sentences: "You're doing a great job. I'll let you know if I have any concerns. Keep up the good work."

In that moment, I realized that I would never receive a comprehensive evaluation from this senior pastor. We had a great relationship, and he was truly pleased with my work, but giving performance reviews was not one of his strengths. So I realized that I needed to reframe my understanding of feedback in light of my first chair's personality.

This meant three specific steps for me. First, I needed to interpret the feedback (or lack thereof) in light of the person. Because my senior pastor gave praise sparingly, I learned to treasure those moments when I did receive recognition. Second, I tried to read between the lines. When he didn't say anything, I took that to mean he was generally pleased with my performance. Occasionally he didn't say anything verbally, but I could sense some kind of frustration or displeasure. That leads to the third step—asking for specifics. If I sensed that my senior pastor was unhappy, I would ask a direct question. Or if I wanted feedback on a particular aspect of my work, I would focus on this. "Can you give me feedback on Tuesday's meeting?" is very different than asking, "How am I doing in my job?" You are more likely to get meaningful feedback if the topic is well defined.

Your first chair leader's approach to giving feedback may be completely different. She may be so positive that you would never know if she is unhappy with something. Or he may be just the opposite—always able to find a fault no matter what you do. Regardless of the particular personality or style, these three steps are a good starting point.

But these steps are only a starting point. They are all dependent on your first chair, and your boss is not the only person who can give meaningful feedback. The staff members and the key laypeople you work with can also point out areas where you are most effective and those where you need to grow. With these groups, even more so than with a first chair, your requests will need to be specific. A generic question like "How am I doing?" or even "What do I need to improve?" may result in generic responses that are not constructive. If you ask for their observations on specific points, the conversation will be more productive. You might even use a "360 survey" if you want more extensive feedback.

Another category of others is to seek feedback from people who are not part of your church or ministry. Even though they may not be insiders who observe your regular work, their expertise can be valuable. An outsider can give input on a sermon or on a marketing campaign or on a strategic plan. A coach or a friend who knows you well may be able to ask a penetrating question about an incident even if they were not present.

If feedback—from your first chair and others—is sparse or is not particularly meaningful, you can create your own standard. You are a leader who thinks strategically, so you should have clear ideas about what needs to be done for your church or ministry to accomplish its mission. What is your role in making this happen? Can you translate this into specific goals?

If you can develop concrete goals for the next period of time (i.e., the next quarter or year), then you have a way to evaluate your own performance, and in doing so, to create a sense of personal satisfaction that you have done your job well. Those goals should obviously relate to the church or ministry's overall strategy. Ideally, you would discuss them with your first chair. You might even have a chance to review them with your first chair at the end of the quarter (or year).

Jenny had created the church's first performance-appraisal process in her first year as executive pastor. By the end of her third year, the system seemed to be working and everyone had received a review—everyone except Jenny whose senior pastor was always too busy to complete the form. So Jenny decided to create a set of quarterly goals and to simply ask her senior pastor to affirm them.

Based on the church's needs and its mission, she identified three major priorities: hiring a new director for the children's ministry, creating an onboarding process for new staff members, and working with the missions director to develop local partnerships that would complement their long-standing focus on international missions. These were affirmed in one of her regular meetings with the senior pastor. Of course, these were in addition to her many regular responsibilities, but it provided new focus for her work. And just as important, the accomplishment of these goals over the next three months gave Jenny a sense of fulfillment that was not dependent on recognition from her senior pastor or anyone else.

Jenny's story points out another key element of fulfillment for second chair leaders: learning to celebrate the successes of others. Second chairs need to find satisfaction in knowing that their contributions may be indirect but nevertheless important. When the children's ministry is functioning better than ever and is increasingly aligned with the mission, Jenny can know that a great hiring decision was a key step. When staff morale is high or when new staff members get up to speed quickly, Jenny can recognize that the onboarding process contributed to this. The mission director may be the one to announce the first local partnership, but Jenny can quietly realize that her gentle coaxing is what helped him see the value in this new focus.

How should you think about your own effectiveness? The specific goals will be unique to your context, but let me suggest four categories that are applicable for most second chair leaders:

- *Execution of the strategy and alignment with the mission.* As described in chapter 4, second chair leaders typically oversee the implementation of the vision or strategic plan. This plan should include specific goals or objectives. While these will tend to fall within an individual ministry area, the second chair still has oversight for them. Like Jenny's work with the mission director, the second chair will become more involved in working toward these goals when necessary.

- *Resolution of problems.* There will always be some aspect of a church or ministry that isn't working well. It may be an immediate crisis (a staff member accused of improper conduct) or a smoldering ember (a department that is consistently mediocre). Second chair leaders are problem solvers, so identifying the most important issues and dealing with them effectively is an ongoing part of the job.

- *Staff morale and effectiveness.* Staff management is normally a large part of the job for second chair leaders (see chapter 5), so helping the staff function better is a key indicator of success. Jenny's original development of the performance evaluation process and her subsequent focus on the onboarding process are both examples of this.

- *Overall organizational success.* Second chairs are not in the first chair and don't have the authority of being the lead leader, but they are directly connected to the success of the church or ministry. When things are going well, they should find fulfillment in this, even if they're not getting any credit. If things are not going well, they can't avoid the feeling of defeat and can't help but wonder what they should do differently.

This section has only focused on the first part of Isaiah 49:4. I've addressed ways that a second chair leader can avoid feeling as though he or she has labored to no purpose. I've suggested ways that you can sense that your strength is being spent for something valuable. While this may be important, true fulfillment comes in experiencing the rest of the verse: "my reward is with my God."

The First Step toward the Real Reward

Is this even possible? Can a person feel fulfilled if he or she is experiencing little success (as defined by the world) and sparse affirmation?

For much of my life, my answer to these questions would have been "no." I've always been a high achiever, and like many people on this path, success became a kind of addiction for me. Of course, I would deny this if confronted, but if you put me in an environment where I wasn't meeting a goal or overcoming a challenge, you wouldn't have seen me thriving.

The first step in recovery from any kind of addiction is to admit that you have a problem, and over the past decade or so, a number of voices have begun to reshape my understanding of success. I once asked Greg Hawkins, who was the executive pastor at Willow Creek for a number of years, how he dealt with setbacks and "failures." He responded, "By whose standard did it fail? God never said, 'Do this because it will work.' He said, 'Do it because you want to obey me.'"

This kind of obedience, even when "results" are not evident, has been a characteristic of Christian heroes through the centuries. The prophet Jeremiah was unable to spark a revival in the nation of Judah. Even though he saw his predictions come to pass, this is one time that "I told you so" couldn't have been any consolation. William Wilberforce spent much of his adult life, not to mention his resources and reputation, trying to abolish slavery in England. While the tide turned during his lifetime, the final bill didn't pass Parliament until just days before his death. We speak of missionary Jim Elliott with great respect today, but after four years in the South American jungles, he was killed with few converts to his credit. We have the benefit of looking back through the long lens of history and celebrating their impact, but in the midst of their journeys, these individuals must have often felt like failures.

Faithful obedience is a much different standard for success than the one found in the world. Unfortunately, the "world" often includes colleagues and influencers in ministry. The very people who should be helping us define success as faithful obedience have often adopted language that sounds like a Wall Street press release. The corporate focus on whether this quarter's numbers are up compared to last quarter or an executive's big promotion has more influence on ministry leaders than we want to admit.

I am not suggesting that we should ignore numerical results or other typical measures of organizational effectiveness. If these indicators are headed in a negative direction, it is appropriate for a leader to ask why. Leaders must be willing to look honestly at the facts and ask the hard questions.

I am, however, saying that one voice should matter far more than any other. When ministry leaders go to bed at the end of a long day, do they sense the Spirit of God saying, "Well done, good and faithful servant" (Matt 25:21)? This emphasizes faithfulness far more than productivity. I don't believe that the Spirit will say, "Contributions are down by 2 percent this month—you need to do better!"

I reconnected with Blake, a pastor I had not seen for a couple of years. He had served in several second chair roles before becoming the solo pastor of a small church. As we talked, he described his internal struggle with defining success. When Blake talked with other ministry colleagues, it seemed that they always ended up asking when he would move to his next church. The implication was that following God always resulted in climbing the career ladder to larger churches. But Blake didn't sense any nudging from the Spirit to leave.

Fortunately, he resisted those other voices and continued his fruitful ministry in his church.

Second chair leaders often experience an even more intense form of this pressure. Not only are they subject to the comparison game, many of their peers think that the second chair role is just an intermediate point on the journey, never a calling. The "when will you move?" question seems to hang in the air whenever they are with ministry colleagues.

One of the "aha" moments in my journey occurred when I read Ruth Haley Barton's *Strengthening the Soul of the Leader*. This powerful book based on the life of Moses will challenge any success-addicted leader. A pivotal segment of the book considers the final chapter in Moses's life as he stands on Mount Nebo, looking out over the Promised Land—a land that he will never enter. Barton points out that Moses doesn't argue with God, and she concludes that in this moment, he was at peace with himself and with God. Barton offers this question for every Christian leader to consider: "Is it possible for a leader to have encountered God so richly that no matter what we are working toward here on this earth, we know we already have what we most deeply want—the presence of God, that which can never be taken from us?"[1]

As with any kind of addiction, I can't say that I'm cured. I can only say that I'm in recovery. Barton says, "As we stay faithful to the journey into the center of our being where God dwells, . . . we are less and less mesmerized by human voices, less and less manipulated by the expectations of others and more and more given over to God."[2] It is a journey. So if the first step is to acknowledge our problem, what are the next steps we need to take?

Deeper Steps

Like most parents, we had lengthy conversations about how much and what kind of media our children should be exposed to when they were young. We were (and still are) convinced that watching the wrong kinds of messages would affect their thinking, and that absorbing the right kinds of messages could have long-lasting, positive impacts.

At the risk of being labeled as simplistic or even insulting, the most important step that you can take to experience deeper, true fulfillment is to spend more

1. Ruth Haley Barton, *Strengthening the Soul of Your Leadership: Finding God in the Crucible of Ministry* (Downers Grove, IL: InterVarsity Press, 2008), 215.

2. Ibid.

time with God. Spend time reflecting on Scripture and communing with God in prayer. Push away from the many forms of garbage that try to influence your thinking, and draw toward the Creator who loves you and wants to be in a growing relationship with you.

Why am I offering such "remedial" advice? While I don't know you personally, I have spent enough time with second chair leaders to be confident in my general diagnosis. Ministry leaders tend to spend lots of time talking about God but relatively little time being with God. They may "do God's work" all day long but leave little time for God to work on them. I see this with young and old leaders, with ones who are in all different kinds of roles, with those who are seminary trained and those whose background is in the marketplace.

If you're skeptical, let me offer a few diagnostic questions for your personal reflection. How much time do you spend each day and week reading Scripture for no purpose other than to allow God to speak to you? This excludes studying for your next sermon or Bible study, or looking for an answer to the question posed by a church member. How much time do you spend praying alone? Not in a hospital room or a church prayer meeting or the start of a committee meeting. Just you and God. Do you have long, uninterrupted times for prayer where you can truly listen to what the Spirit may be saying? Or do your times for prayer come in short spurts between meetings or walking out the door or sitting in traffic? When was the last time you had at least a half day (and preferably a full day or two) to get away so that you could listen and reflect more deeply on what God might want to say to you? Perhaps you nailed this "test." (If you think of it as a test, you're probably still struggling with an addiction to achievement.) If the practices listed above accurately describe you and your relationship with God, you may find that it's not hard to tune out the siren cry of success and to focus on faithful obedience. On the other hand, these questions may reveal that you need to make some shifts.

One of the turning points in my journey was a brief story I read many years ago. The author had determined that an early morning time with God needed to be treated as his most important appointment of the day. When he thought about his job, he realized that he wouldn't miss appointments unless there was an emergency. Why should God be less important than clients or colleagues? So he "scheduled" his appointment with God early each morning. That meant changing his evening routine so that he could get a good night's sleep and be ready for his first "meeting." He was even known to leave guests in his living room, explaining that he needed to go to bed in order to be ready for an early appointment the next morning.

After reading that story, I quit watching the evening news and the talk shows that came on afterward, and I started going to bed earlier. I also changed my morning routine. Whereas in the past, I had always exercised right after I got up, I decided that I could not exercise until after spending time with God. For some, that might not be a motivation, but since I love to exercise, this was an important step for me.

I don't know what the key is for you. I'm not suggesting a specific formula or even a "best" time of day. But I am certain that you won't experience deep satisfaction apart from a meaningful and consistent experience with the only One whose commendation of "Well done, good and faithful servant" will penetrate to the depths of your soul.

Spending time with God is the only antidote to the flood of contrary messages that we receive on a daily basis. Whether it's a carefully crafted ad on TV or a casual comment by a colleague, there are many sources that claim to hold the secret to a rich, fulfilled life. We need a big dose of godly wisdom to counteract these seductive ideas.

Doug's breakthrough moment came on a retreat. The speaker led them through a series of passages in Scripture and exercises to reflect on their true identity. Doug soaked up this teaching like a dry sponge being placed in water. The words that kept ringing in his mind and settling in his soul were "beloved child of God." He realized that this was God's truth, and that this identity was far more important than anything he might accomplish in his second chair role. As he embraced this identity, it became easier for him to say "no" to demands by church members. He spent more time with his family, without feeling guilty for "neglecting" his church, and he developed new self-care habits. He cherished his daily time with God, where the message of "beloved child" was reinforced. And he began to lead differently, encouraging staff members toward a deeper spiritual walk.

Pressure from others—both subtle and not-so-subtle—can be powerful, but the biggest enemy in our pursuit of true fulfillment is often the person in the mirror. Ruth Haley Barton says, "In our encounters with God we die not only to the expectations of others but also to ourselves—our addictions to performing, to looking good and being perfect, to attaining more status than is good for us."[3] Each of us has choices to make in how we describe ourselves, and those outward descriptions often influence our internal identity.

One friend had been a successful businesswoman before choosing to be a stay-at-home mom. She was confident in this decision, until she began bumping

3. Ibid., 210.

into former colleagues who asked what she was doing. They often put the dreaded "just" in front of her status—"just a stay-at-home mom." So she developed a different way to introduce her new role—"I'm training two young men who will be future Christian leaders." There is no "just" at the start of that description.

You may hear—or even say—"just" to describe what you do. "Just" an associate or "just" serving this less-than-prominent church. Stop doing that. If you are being faithful to God's call in your life, then you don't need to add a "just." You don't need to feel like a failure. Second chair does not mean second class.

These stories point to another important truth for any leader who lives in the swirl of godly and less-than-godly messages. We can't eliminate the presence of negative or demeaning ideas and identities. But we can, to some extent, choose what we filter out and what we let in. One of the most effective filters is choosing who you spend time with.

You may think that you really don't have much choice in this. You can't ignore members of your congregation or change the people you work with or avoid colleagues when you go to a training event or denominational meeting. While that may be true, you can choose how much time you spend with them and what you talk about. You can decide who you go to dinner with during a conference. You can decide who you will seek out for advice. If a friend starts talking about climbing the career ladder, you can listen politely for a few minutes and then redirect the conversation.

Just as you can choose to filter out unhelpful voices, you can make conscious choices to invite others to speak into your life. Finding those human voices that offer godly counsel and wisdom will help you resist the world's competing messages. They can ask the hard questions that will challenge your motivations or that will help you rediscover your true identity.

Hearing and following God's voice is the ultimate way to thrive, not only in a second chair career, but in all of life. God is the one who can turn "the desert into pools of water and the parched ground into flowing springs" (Ps 107:35). His voice will assure you that your labors are not in vain. It will rise above the silence of a less-than-appreciative first chair or the attacks of a critic. It will shine light on the path of faithful obedience for you to follow. And when God's voice is echoed in the words of faith-filled friends, you'll discover a lifeline for overcoming loneliness and continuing to thrive.

Personal Reflection

- How do you define success for your role? If it hasn't been defined for you, then create your own standard.
- Does it bother you that it's hard to put a finger on success in the second chair? How are you dealing with this?
- What is the Holy Spirit saying to you through the two statements by Ruth Haley Barton on page 119?
- How is it with your soul? Honestly evaluate the state of your spiritual practices and your relationship with God. What do you need to change?

Discuss with Your First Chair

- First chairs: How do you define "success" for your second chair?
- Second chairs: What ideas from this chapter resonated the most with you? Share with your first chair any commitments you are making, particularly related to your spiritual growth.
- How can you support and encourage each other toward deeper faith and greater dependence on God?

Chapter 9

Overcome Loneliness

Second chair leaders thrive by forming safe relationships with trusted peers that provide camaraderie and wise counsel.

We've visited eight of the springs so far, and this leads to an important question: When you are struggling to find any of the previous sources that can quench your thirst for thriving—and there will be times when finding them seems impossible—who do you talk to? Who can you confide in at a deep level, sharing whatever frustrations or failures or doubts that you may be experiencing? Who knows you well enough to be a great conversation partner? Who understands this unique second chair role sufficiently that they can relate to your challenges? Who has earned your trust enough to hold up a mirror and point out things that you have not seen about yourself?

Many second chair leaders don't have confident, positive answers to these questions. You may be surrounded by people, and you may have many friends, but these individuals don't measure up to the standard that these questions suggest. If you are really honest and look into the depths of your soul, you may realize that you're feeling lonely in the second chair.

Not Alone, but Lonely

The e-mails started a few weeks after *Leading from the Second Chair* was released. One person said, "I'm a second chair leader and have felt lost, frustrated, and alone out here in this world of second chair." Another expressed, "I've known that I lead from the second chair, but have never heard it validated or talked about. THANK YOU!" A third said, "I wept throughout the entire book. Someone finally put words to my role in the body of Christ.... I wasn't crazy after all."

We realized that we had tapped into something deep, much deeper and more widespread than we had expected. Researchers have documented the isolation felt by many ministry leaders, but it was clear that second chairs were experiencing a different kind of loneliness. They truly felt that they had no one to talk to. As we had more and more conversations, it became clear that they needed more than just a book.

Why do second chair leaders often feel "lost, frustrated, and alone"? One of the reasons is that they have few true peers. If a second chair leader goes to a typical conference or a denominational meeting, he or she may have to search diligently to find others in similar roles. The participants will include many first chair leaders plus others who are specialists in particular areas (worship, children, youth, missions). Some may be in second chair roles but will make it clear that they're just passing through on the way to the first chair. Few will say that they are called to (or at least planning to spend considerable time in) the second chair. Of course, the programming for this event will reflect the roles of the participants, which means that second chair leaders may find little that directly relates to their jobs.

In addition to the lack of true peers, second chairs often find that their roles are misunderstood by others. As mentioned in the previous chapter, this is expressed in a casual comment that "she is 'just' a second chair leader" or a well-meaning question such as, "What exactly do you do?" Sometimes the second chair's role is so much behind the scenes that they feel invisible even to the leaders within their own church or ministry.

This lack of understanding often translates into a lack of relevant advice. In those moments when thriving is elusive, a second chair longs for a listening ear and wise counsel. But even the wisdom offered by trusted friends may miss the mark.

Terry, who served in an executive pastor role, had been looking forward to the annual denominational gathering for weeks. Not that he enjoyed the formal programming that consisted of too many boring reports and internal debates. His excitement stemmed from the opportunity that he would have to spend time with Craig. The two had been close friends in seminary and were always able to pick up right where they left off whenever they reconnected. Like Terry, Craig was serving in a large church in a suburban area. But unlike Terry, Craig's primary role was to lead the church's extensive mission ministry, which included multiple local and international partnerships.

Over dinner, Terry began sharing about the tension that had developed between him and his senior pastor. Terry explained, "It's hard to put a finger on it. He never tells me that he's unhappy. But I had almost no input in the decision about the new Sunday schedule. And he has been spending a lot of time with the youth ministry team, trying to get their program turned around, even though they report to me."

Craig listened closely as Terry finished. It was obvious that his friend was upset and looking for advice. Craig thought about his own struggles with a demanding senior pastor. He responded, "I understand. Even though we've added three new partnerships this year, I feel like I'm never meeting my senior pastor's expectations. I've realized that the best thing to do is just to put my head down and work hard, and not involve him in my ministry any more than necessary."

Terry walked back to his hotel room that night feeling more alone than before. Even his good friend and ministry colleague didn't get it. In Terry's role, it really wasn't an option to just put his head down and work hard. His ability to lead effectively was completely dependent on his relationship with his senior pastor and the authority that was extended through that relationship.

Dangerous Disclosure

Somewhere in your second chair journey, you may have had an experience like Terry. And while this is frustrating and disappointing, Terry's decision to wait and talk to Craig avoided one of the major mistakes of loneliness—dangerous disclosure. Dangerous disclosure occurs when a second chair leader's frustrations spill out to a person who shouldn't hear them.

For second chair leaders, the list of people to whom they shouldn't disclose their frustrations is far longer than the list of safe and helpful individuals. You might start with the first chair leader. In a great partnership, the first chair can be a valuable conversation partner. But what about the times when the first chair is the source of, or at least a contributor to, the problem? Of course, second chairs eventually need to work through any relational stresses with their first chairs, but that may be a second step after first finding someone else to talk with. Even if the first-second chair relationship isn't strained, it often feels inappropriate to "unload" on first chair leaders who are already burdened with their own challenges.

If not the first chair, it may seem natural to look around at other people within your church or ministry. They know you and understand the context, so they may have great insights. But it is rarely appropriate to draw them into these conversations. Within the staff, second chair leaders may not have any true peers. Discussing a situation with a fellow staff member may actually mean venting to a subordinate, and this is the kind of disclosure that can quickly become dangerous.

What about lay leaders? If you are seeking their input on an issue where they have expertise and/or responsibility, then this is probably an appropriate conversation. The intersection between their leadership responsibilities and yours is a natural point of interaction, as described in chapter 7. It's appropriate (in most cases) to talk to the finance chair about your concerns that the deficit is larger than expected. But if you're actually frustrated that the music director has overspent his budget by 30 percent and that the senior pastor is unwilling to rein him in, you need to tread carefully. That's the point at which you've gone beyond your role and stepped onto thin ice.

This points to the central issue for many lonely second chair leaders. When they have a great relationship with their first chairs, they rarely experience the depths of loneliness. They are most likely to feel lonely because there is a point of tension with their first chair. A conversation with an insider, if it relates to this tension, can easily start down the slope toward insubordination. That is why I added the parenthetical "in most cases" in the previous paragraph. Where is the conversation about the budget deficit going to lead? If it will end up focusing on the senior pastor—a lax attitude toward spending or an unwillingness to teach on stewardship—then it's a conversation to avoid.

How do you know when it is appropriate to talk with those inside your church or ministry? Two simple guidelines will help, one that applies before you start the conversation and one that will help you end the conversation when necessary. Imagine that an unbiased third person is listening to your discussion. What would she observe? Would she tell you that it sounds insubordinate or divisive? Or imagine your first chair overhearing what you said. How would he react? If you don't like what you imagine, don't even start the conversation with an insider.

Second, what about the cases where the conversation takes an unanticipated turn? You may simply want to inform the finance chair about the deficit, and she starts asking hard questions about the senior pastor. That's where the second guideline comes in. Don't get caught up in triangulation. If the discussion shifts in this way, support your first chair as much as you can. Then encourage the other person to have a direct conversation with your first chair, not to use you as an intermediary. In most cases, you should then give your first chair a heads-up about the concern and how you responded.

Shannon had been troubled for over a year about the downward trends in all of the ministry's statistical indicators. By virtue of her role as associate director and her reputation as the numbers person, she watched these details closely. At times, she felt as though she was the only one who paid attention. From her perspective, the ministry needed to make some bold moves, but the executive director (first chair) seemed more inclined to maintain the status quo. Then the finance chair surprised Shannon at the end of one of their quarterly meetings. After Shannon had pointed out the declines, the chair responded, "I've noticed this. Are other ministries in our area experiencing similar trends, or is this a leadership issue?" Shannon had a definite opinion on this question, but rather than answering, she suggested that the finance chair talk to the director. It was a near miss with dangerous disclosure.

There is one other "insider" who is a very special case—the spouse of the second chair leader. When you are in the midst of a difficult season, how much should you disclose to your husband or wife? I am reluctant to answer this question, because each marriage is different. A great we-talk-about-everything marriage is a powerful antidote to the isolation that many second chair leaders experience. So let me simply offer two cautions. First, it's risky to hide things from your spouse. If things are not going well in your work, it will inevitably be noticed at home. Saying "everything is fine," when it's obviously not, is likely to create distance in your marriage. Second, beware of the opposite risk of over-disclosure. Once a spouse is in-the-know, he or she may find it more difficult to engage in worship or to respect the first chair. It may generate anxiety for them, worrying that today's problems could result in tomorrow's job termination.

So far, I've warned you against talking to friends who are insiders. Are there any exceptions? In some cases, a second chair has a longstanding relationship with a leader in the church or ministry who is completely trustworthy and very mature. This person knows the second chair and the context. He or she listens well and is not reactive. They don't jump in to "fix" the problem on your behalf. When the second chair vents, they listen a lot, give a little advice, don't feel obliged to act, and never repeat what has been said. It's a very high standard. If you have that kind of person in your life, consider yourself blessed.

If you generally can't turn to "insiders," what about those who are outside of your church or ministry? As we saw in Terry's case, even a friend such as Craig may listen closely but not really understand the dynamics of the situation. The second chair truly is a unique role that few people can relate to. Even denominations that create systems designed to support clergy are often puzzled by how to handle the second chair as a career. It is certainly safer to voice your frustrations with an outsider, but you may be disappointed in the counsel you receive. Just as it is rare to find a safe and helpful insider, the outsider who can fully share the journey is a special blessing.

Unfortunately, that leaves many second chair leaders in a difficult place. When the stress mounts, they may violate one of the guidelines by venting their concerns to a fellow staff member or an unprepared lay leader, or they may dump all their garbage on their spouse. Or they may bury it, deciding that they can't talk to anyone and they are strong enough to deal with it on their own.

As with any other kind of deep stress, stuffing down emotions may be the most dangerous response of all because these feelings will eventually resurface, often at the most inopportune time. Some people implode slowly. They develop physical ailments or have problems sleeping. They lose their energy for work and family or find that their decision-making becomes fuzzy. They may turn to addictive or inappropriate behavior to numb their pain. Others explode. It may be at home or at the office and may or may not be directed at the source of their stress. One way or another, deep and unresolved stress will come out.

None of these stress-triggered outcomes are pretty. But you may be wondering if they can be avoided. It may seem as though you've been painted into a corner with no easy ways to escape the challenge of loneliness. So let me offer a way out.

Draw Near

As I began to better understand the depths and dangers of the loneliness challenge, I changed the conclusion of my seminars on second chair leadership. While each workshop is different, I often close with this advice: "Draw near to God, to your first chair, and to other second chairs." It's obvious that drawing near to God is essential, as we saw in the previous chapter. A vibrant spiritual life can overcome deficiencies in any of the other practices for thriving. Likewise, a trust-based relationship with your first chair leader creates a partnership that overcomes many of the other second chair challenges and prevents loneliness.

So how important is it to draw near to other second chairs? Is this a relationship that is "nice to have," or is it also a vital component for thriving? I believe it's the latter. It's not as important as your relationship with God or with your first chair, but I rank it ahead of all the other springs for thriving. It is those "other second chairs" who can best relate to and understand the unique challenges and pressures of your role. Unlike Craig in the earlier story, they know that a healthy relationship with the first chair is needed and that you can't "just put your head down and work." They understand the inner turmoil that you experience as you try to decide how to deal with a complicated personnel issue. They've felt completely overwhelmed by "urgent" priorities. And they've experienced loneliness as well.

When you are truly known by people who understand you and your role, they can offer a safe place for you to share your deepest difficulties and anxieties. They can give wise counsel on how you might mend a strained relationship with your first chair or how to address some other challenge. They may lovingly help you see places where you've been in the wrong or where you need to change. In moments when you don't need advice, they can listen well, helping you sort through the myriad of feelings you have. They can point you toward God and pray for you.

"I'm pretty sure that I'm going to kill him. Or he's going to kill me." Those were Sonya's introductory words when she met with a group of executive pastors. This was their sixth meeting, and during that time they had grown very close. One of the others asked, "Who is 'him'?" but they already knew the answer was almost certain to be Sonya's senior pastor, Nick. As the story unfolded, Sonya described Nick's penchant for jumping into the middle of things and making changes after ministry plans were far down the road. Sonya kept finding herself in the middle, trying to be a loyal executive pastor but also protecting her staff from Nick's unbridled spontaneity. Shortly before the group meeting, Nick had told Sonya to "quit being a wet blanket every time that I have a good idea." Sonya's friends were able to offer counsel on alternatives for dealing with this situation. But more importantly, they listened and prayed for Sonya, and gave her the encouragement she needed to not give up.

Getting to this point isn't quick or easy. Not only do you have to invest consistently in building these relationships, you also have to be willing to take some risks and let your guard down. This is a far cry from the typical drill when ministry leaders gather. Everyone follows an invisible script in which they talk about all the good things that have been happening in their church or ministry.

The numbers are up or have just turned a corner. The staff is great. The anecdotal stories of changed lives abound. And the individuals who are struggling play the game outwardly, while inwardly thinking that no one in this conversation can relate to their issues.

In reality, many of the people in that conversation can relate. But someone has to go first. Someone has to be willing to say, "Things aren't going that well. We launched a major initiative to reverse our downward trend, and it failed. The only result was more conflict. On top of that, I think that we need to get two people off the bus, but I can't convince my first chair to act, and it's causing a lot of tension between us."

I'm not recommending that you blurt this out in a group when you first meet them at a conference or denominational gathering. There's a term for this, and it's not "transparency"—it's over-sharing. You can, however, identify a person or a small group with whom you would like to go deeper. Imagine moving beyond that superficial conversation by telling one or two second chair acquaintances that you'd enjoy getting to know them better and learning how they do their jobs. Over coffee or dinner, you can begin to talk about the real joys and struggles. You can see if this leads to a deeper, ongoing relationship.

You may be wondering, "Where do I find these people? In my denomination or town, I don't think that anyone else does what I do." Strictly speaking, you may be correct. That's why you will probably need to draw the circle bigger. The issues that second chair leaders face are widely shared. They cut across denominational and theological lines. They may look slightly different for clergy versus non-clergy, but dig a little deeper, and the differences aren't as large as they may have appeared. There is even great similarity between those who are in local churches and the second chairs in other kinds of ministry settings. When you find someone who is truly a peer in ministry and who is willing to be honest about their highs and lows, you may have found a person to draw near to.

One of the specific ways of drawing near to other second chairs is to form a group that will meet together on a regular basis. For almost ten years, I have had the privilege of leading these kinds of groups, primarily through the Texas Methodist Foundation (TMF). TMF's Leadership Ministry has formed a variety of learning communities for ministry leaders. Their groups for second chair leaders have been comprised of truly exceptional people from large United Methodist churches in Texas and beyond. It is an environment where iron sharpens iron and where gifted leaders develop new capacities that enable them to steward their own potential and that of their churches.

It is also an environment that has been safe and supportive for the members, which is one of the most important factors for second chair leaders who are looking for meaningful peer relationships. Group members have worked through difficult staff issues, organizational upheaval, strained relationships with senior pastors, and questions of whether they should leave their current places of ministry. These are the kinds of issues that require the utmost confidentiality and that often cause second chairs to feel alone. We have laughed and shed tears together, and have prayed for each other many times. And on a consistent basis, someone in the group has said, "I don't know where else I could turn to find this kind of counsel and support."

You may not have a TMF that will create a group for you, but you don't have to remain isolated. You can take the initiative to gather other second chair leaders, thinking broadly as suggested above. It may be as simple as inviting several people to lunch and then seeing if there is enough mutual interest to continue meeting.

Even though this section has emphasized drawing near to other second chair leaders, those are not the only relationships that can provide wise counsel and an empathetic ear. Someone within your church or ministry may have the emotional maturity and personality to hear your struggles without overreacting or breaching your confidentiality. You may be blessed with a spouse who can play a valuable role by walking alongside you in tough seasons. Beyond this, some ministry friends, even if they've never been in a second chair position, may know you well enough and understand the organizational dynamics sufficiently to provide great support. An increasing number of ministry leaders are also turning to coaches to help them grow in their leadership and work through thorny dilemmas.

As you consider where you might turn to develop these relationships, one other thought may cross your mind: "This sounds like it will take a lot of effort. I can't afford the time." I don't doubt that your calendar is full and that your list of things to do seems endless. But I will challenge your claim that you don't have time. We make time for the things that are most important to us. And I don't believe that you can afford to not invest in life-giving relationships that will overcome loneliness. The cost of living in isolation and not thriving is simply too high.

The Power of Friends

A chapter from my journey illustrates the power of having these kinds of rich relationships. Vocational ministry was a second career for me, and it was one that

I embraced. I was confident that God had called me into the role that evolved into an executive pastor position. And while I knew that God could call me to a different place, I envisioned that I might stay in that role and at my church until I retired.

But along the way, things began to change. We made changes in leadership, in the organization, and in the strategy. I found myself on a different page from my senior pastor more often and feeling satisfied in my role less often. I questioned whether my gifts and passions fit our church's future needs and direction. I wondered if God was leading me to a new chapter of ministry. And I desperately needed people who could help me make sense of all of this.

Fortunately, I found them. Actually, I already had the relationships and was able to draw on them in this time of need. I was blessed by a church member who was a wise, trusted friend. I knew he would keep my confidences and that he would not try to fix the problem for me. I also knew he would have keen insights into our church and into my temperament. He helped me to see through the fog and evaluate my gifts more clearly in light of the church's current and future needs.

One denominational leader had known me for many years, and I was able to approach him as a friend. Even though he didn't know our church well, he had a great understanding of congregational dynamics. Through several conversations with him, I began to develop a perspective on the organizational changes that didn't focus on "right" or "wrong" but simply defined reality in a more objective way. He also helped me see what the future might look like for me if I decided to stay.

I also reached out to a coach who had previously been an executive pastor. He helped me find the language to describe the emotions I was feeling, which then gave me healthier ways to deal with them. Since he had successfully transitioned out of a second chair role, our conversations began to reveal a viable path and enabled me to think of possibilities beyond my role.

During this season, TMF's second chair group was a vital part of my network of advice and encouragement. They allowed me to be both their leader and a peer in ministry. They had the experience in second chair roles and the relationship with me that allowed them to ask penetrating questions that revealed my blind spots, inaccurate assumptions, and growth areas. It's a delicate balance to offer probing insight and needed encouragement, but that is exactly what they did.

And throughout this season, I was blessed beyond measure in my true partnership with my wife. She knows me better than anyone else. She always had the right words and the right questions at the right times, including no words in those times when I just needed someone to listen. Even though it was not an easy season for her, and my decision was going to have major implications for all of our family, she didn't focus on her needs or feelings. And when it became increasingly clear that God was pointing me toward the exit, she gave me permission (and even a gentle nudge) to jump.

I write this not as a prescription but to demonstrate the power that is available to overcome loneliness. I am not suggesting that all difficult seasons end with a second chair leaving. I've seen many cases where just the opposite is the case. They work through challenges and often reinvent themselves within their roles, a subject that will be the focus of the next chapter. For me, it became clear that my season as an executive pastor at our church was closing and that God was opening a new door for the consulting and coaching ministry that I continue to do. But as I look back, I'm certain that the decision would not have been as clear if I had not had this incredible community upon which to draw.

I am notoriously hard headed, so I'm glad that I had so many friends to share the journey with. You may not need such a large cast of characters. You may only need one person. But do you have that person—or those people—in your life? That person with whom you truly can share anything and from whom you can draw wonderful, life-giving, godly wisdom. Or let me ask the question in a different way. Do you have at least one person who truly knows you and who is praying for you and with you? Whether or not you have this relationship today, I hope you will make it a priority to draw near to God and to others.

Personal Reflection

- In what ways are you at risk of "dangerous disclosure"?
- Do you have trusted friends who know you and can give wise counsel related to your second chair role?
- If not, make a list of people you can reach out to, either individually or to explore the possibility of a second chair group. Don't just make the list—begin to connect with them.

Discuss with Your First Chair

- Discuss any concerns about disclosure that may have been out of bounds.
- Second chairs: Share with your first chair your plan for connecting with other second chairs. How can your first chair support you and hold you accountable?

Chapter 10

Extend Your "Shelf Life"

Reinventing their roles offers a way for second chair leaders to thrive and be reenergized.

"Does a second chair leader have a shelf life?" The question caught me by surprise. I had never thought about the idea that a person's effectiveness in the second chair might have an expiration date. This idea suggests that a second chair leader comes into the role to do a job—which might take a number of years—and then eventually gets stale like a loaf of bread on the shelf at the grocery store.

If this is true, it presents a dilemma for second chair leaders: stick around despite decreasing impact and satisfaction, or leave. But these are not the only options. In their best-selling book *Decisive,* the Heath brothers (Chip and Dan) refer to this as "narrow framing."[1] It's what happens when someone *narrows* a decision down to a simple "whether or not" or "yes or no" choice.

The second chair leader who feels stagnant or burned out can easily fall victim to narrow framing by asking, "Is it time for me to leave?" This closed-ended question seems to offer only two choices—yes or no, stay or go. The Heaths say it's a mistake to ask the question this way. Instead, it's important to "widen your options." But what are those wider options? Is it possible to extend your shelf life?

1. Chip Heath and Dan Heath, *Decisive: How to Make Better Choices in Life and Work* (New York: Crown Publishing, 2013), chapter 1.

Beyond an "Expiration Date"

Before exploring the wider options, it is important to understand the factors that can lead second chairs to conclude that they've reached their expiration date. One of the most frequent occurrences is *project completion*. Even though second chair leaders are generalists, it is not uncommon for them to be brought into the role to solve a specific problem or work on a major project. These are not small, garden-variety problems or projects that can be knocked out in a few months but instead are ministry-wide, long-term priorities.

After several years of rapid growth, the leaders of one parachurch ministry recognized that their processes and systems were inadequate. They hired Kate, a seasoned business leader, into the new role of associate director with the charge to "get everything running so that we can do our ministry more effectively." She led the team in the implementation of a new database, personnel policies and procedures, program monitoring, budgeting, and more. She ran hard for three years, barely slowing down to catch her breath. At a staff retreat shortly before her fourth anniversary, Kate had a chance to reflect on all they had accomplished. While there was still work to be done, she felt a great sense of satisfaction at the progress they had made and how well things were running. By the end of the retreat, however, a nagging doubt had entered her mind: What's next?

Completing a major overhaul of internal systems is just one way that a second chair may sense a personal expiration date due to project completion. That same feeling can be triggered when a strategic plan comes to fruition or when construction on a new building is finished. It can occur for the second chair who entered the picture to clean up a messy staff situation, moving some into new roles, helping others exit, changing the organizational structure, and filling key positions. During this season, it seems that the second chair is always doing his job and covering the vacancies. And once the new staff is assembled and up to speed, the second chair may wonder: What now?

Some kind of pause is inevitable when a massive, multiyear initiative is completed. Catching one's breath and stopping to reflect are not causes for staleness unless this is coupled with a lack of new challenges or a less-than-exciting vision for the future. "What's next?" is a great question for any second chair leader to ask periodically, but it's a problem if they don't like what they see or hear in response.

This brings us back to vision, or more precisely, the short shelf life that can be caused by an absence of vision. Second chair leaders may push back when a vision seems completely detached from reality, as noted in chapter 2. But they do want to be challenged, and they quickly grow stale when they're not. A vision that inspires and stretches them is essential. It insures that there will be fresh ways that they can use their leadership and organizational gifts to pursue Kingdom work.

An under-challenged second chair leader is like a thoroughbred horse that is sold to a farmer and harnessed to a plow. It's not a pretty picture, and it's not good stewardship of a valuable resource. When this happens, second chairs may take much-needed vacations and slow down for a few weeks, but then they will start to get fidgety. They may meddle in areas that don't need help. They may initiate something that seems to be a natural extension of the mission, but in doing so may overstep their authority. Or they may simply conclude that their time at a particular church or ministry is done.

Shelf-life concerns can also arise when second chair leaders feel that too much of their time is spent in areas for which they are not gifted, while some of their abilities are left dormant. Of course, no one knowingly takes a job that is a poor match with their gifts. So how does this happen? One common culprit is what I refer to as "role creep."

"Scope creep" is a term from the field of project management. It refers to the tendency for the scope of a project to gradually expand (or "creep") to the point that the final project is much larger than originally intended. It's what happens when a straightforward sanctuary renovation project is expanded to include "minor updates" to the music suite and the nearby restrooms and the lobby area, plus an upgrade to the sound and projection system. The final result may be wonderful, except that the price tag doubles. Role creep is very similar, but on a personal level.

Role creep can be one of a second chair leader's great enemies. Second chair leaders are often talented, versatile individuals. That's one of the reasons they were hired. They're able to see the big picture, which means that they notice organizational gaps that need to be plugged. And whether they take the initiative on their own or a request is made by the first chair (or board), second chair leaders often find themselves doing all sorts of things that weren't part of their original job description. Along the way, they may give up some of the duties that are most meaningful and fulfilling to them.

Lee is a classic example of how role creep can squeeze the joy out of a second chair. When he stepped into the second chair role, he told his senior pastor that he loved the pastoral aspects of ministry and didn't want to "just be an administrator." Lee saw the executive pastor job as a chance to shape the overall direction of ministry in the church and to be a pastor to the other pastors and programming staff. To stay connected with ministry, he planned to continue sharing pastoral care duties and teaching a Bible study. This is exactly how his role began, but over time, he spent more and more time on administrative tasks and had to squeeze in time for pastoral work. Even his interactions with staff became primarily supervisory rather than pastoral.

Second chair leaders who fall victim to role creep often experience a satisfaction drain. Even if the overall church or ministry is thriving, it's difficult to feel personal fulfillment when this happens. It's not uncommon for a pastor to think, *This isn't why I entered the ministry*. But the issue isn't limited to clergy. Any second chair leader can find that the job has morphed so much over time that it no longer matches their greatest gifts.

"Morph" and "creep" both point to the reality that these changes usually happen in gradual and subtle ways. It's a temporary assignment that somehow becomes permanent. It's the small task that "no one else can do." It can happen when a new team member (who is a welcome addition) ends up taking a life-giving task off of a second chair's plate so that he can focus on other priorities. Any of the added responsibilities may be relatively small, but they accumulate to the point that the role can become almost unrecognizable from its original design.

Sometimes role creep occurs without taking away those activities that are most fulfilling for a second chair leader. There's a word for this as well: overload. As new duties are added, some second chairs don't let go of the things they most enjoy because they're not letting go of anything. It's like turning on the water to fill the sink. At first, the sink has plenty of capacity for more water. But at some point, you have to open the drain or the water overflows, creating a huge mess.

Many second chair leaders either refuse to open the drain, don't know how to do so, or believe that this is not permissible. Unlike the sink analogy, it is not nearly as obvious when they are nearing their capacity. They can always make a little more time by preparing less for a meeting or a Bible study, giving their staff a little less attention, or taking just one more evening away from family. Like the sink analogy, however, the end result is a mess. It may show up in their personal lives or in the quality of their work. It may not become apparent for months or even years. But the overload that comes from role creep is costly.

Earlier in this section, I said that an under-challenged second chair is like a thoroughbred horse that is hitched to a plow. That may not be the best analogy. The racing life of a thoroughbred is short, and then it is put out to pasture. It's better to think of yourself as a master woodworker who loves to build beautiful furniture and wants to do that until he retires. This craftsman takes pride in his work and experiences great satisfaction when it brings joy to others. If the economy changes, however, and the woodworker is forced to take a job installing prefabricated cabinets in tract homes, he will feel frustrated and under-utilized, regardless of how busy he is. In the same way, an under-challenged second chair may be busy but unhappy.

So if you're feeling dissatisfied for one of these reasons, does that mean it's time to search for a more meaningful place to use your talents? This sounds like the same kind of narrow-framing, yes-or-no question that I started this chapter with, and I still believe it's the wrong question. So what is the "right" question? There are actually several right questions that, taken together, can help extend your shelf life.

Asking the Right Questions

It takes time to reach the point where a second chair leader begins to feel stale or senses a looming personal expiration date. It will take time and reflection on several different questions to extend that shelf life. The right questions are organizational, personal, and spiritual:

- Organizational: What are the greatest need(s) that my church or ministry has at this time? What will most help us to accomplish our mission? In what ways can a second chair leader best facilitate this?

- Personal: What activities most make me come alive? What things seem almost effortless because they fit my talents and passions so well? How do these align with the organizational needs that I identified? What am I doing that is not strategic?

- Spiritual: What do I sense God saying to me right now? Is it possible that I am called to stay, even though I'm not in a season where I feel particularly fulfilled in my job? Is this "expiration date" that I am sensing from God, or is it something that I've created?

Answering the organizational questions is a way of thinking strategically. As described in chapter 4, these questions help a second chair see and act more broadly. The personal questions are just as powerful in widening your perspective and are even more important for extending your shelf life. It may seem that the answers to these questions are obvious, but it's easy to get caught up in the busyness of life and never take time to reflect. Apart from this reflection, you may not realize how much of your time is spent on less-than-strategic activities. You may not be aware of the extent to which you've been affected by role creep.

It's also inevitable that a leader will have blind spots. The personal questions should be addressed with someone you trust and who knows you well. A friend or colleague may have insights about your strengths and weaknesses that will dramatically change the way you see yourself.

One executive pastor felt that he was in the perfect role and couldn't put a finger on the cause of his growing frustration. Then a close friend challenged him with a single question: "Do you really enjoy managing people?" He realized that he only enjoyed it when he was working with high-performers. He lacked the patience and sensitivity to coach less-than-stellar staff members to grow in their abilities. One pivotal question helped him realize the mismatch between his role and his talents and passions.

The organizational and personal questions may reveal a variety of ways that a second chair's gifts and passions align with the needs of the church or ministry. This realization may lead to any number of shelf-life extensions—a redefinition of their role, a shift in their priorities, or simply a renewed energy to keep moving forward. Of course, there will also be times when no intersection seems to exist. That's where the spiritual questions come in. It's possible that the time has come to gracefully exit from a second chair role. But it's also possible that God is saying, "Not now. I still have things to teach you. I want to extend your shelf life."

Shelf Life–Extending Answers

If you talk to a senior pastor who has been in the same church for many years, you're likely to hear an interesting thread. Even though the title has been the same for the entire time, the role has changed dramatically. Some of these changes may have been due to societal shifts, but that is only one factor. Often these role changes were necessitated by the growth of the church. As staff were added and the organization became more complex, a different set of skills, different style of leadership, and different allocation of time were needed.

But if you push the conversation to a deeper level, you may find another factor that is just as important as societal or size-related issues. It's a story of reinvention that was prompted by a growing awareness of their own gifts and passions, and a desire to be true to how God has made them. They realized that trying to fit into someone else's mold for a senior pastor meant ignoring God's unique design for their lives. And over time, they grew in their ability to resist those external pressures and shaped their roles to match this most important reality.

Can a second chair leader do the same thing? While you may not have quite as much role-shaping freedom as a first chair leader, you probably have more than you realize. If a youth director realizes that she doesn't enjoy working with teens, there is little she can do to extend her shelf life in that job. She may find a different position in her current church or transition into a new ministry role elsewhere, but she won't find the flexibility that she needs in the youth job.

When it comes to shelf-life extension, a second chair leader has much more opportunity to flex than a youth director (or any other ministry-specific role). Of course, this opportunity is of no value unless you take advantage of it. And doing so may involve some sort of risk. It may be a risky conversation with your first chair or the perception by others that you've taken a step backward. In my experience, the perceived cost is often far worse than reality. Besides, isn't it worth paying a price or taking a risk if that's what is needed for you to thrive?

Shelf life–extending opportunities are as varied as the second chair leaders reading this book and the churches and ministries in which they serve. However, they can be grouped into three broad categories: saying "no," saying "yes," and reimagining fully.

Saying "No"

If role creep and the overload that often comes with it are constantly lurking enemies of thriving, then it seems clear that the answer is to say "no." Of course, it's never that simple or clear, because there are many different circumstances where you need to say "no" and many different ways of doing so.

The easiest, and yet often hardest, is to say "no" to those activities that clearly do not align with your abilities and priorities. It may be the invitation to show up at every single church gathering or to attend certain meetings just because you're the boss or you "always have a good perspective." These are the easiest because you know what your answer should be. They can be the hardest because your own feelings of guilt or self-worth somehow keep the "no" from being verbalized. Conquering this demon requires self-examination, greater awareness, and often an accountability partner who will challenge you to say "no" more often.

At other times, the answer isn't quite as obvious. When a real need exists and you have the ability to meet that need, it is difficult to say "no." In those moments, the opening words of Jim Collins's classic book *Good to Great* should echo in your mind: "Good is the enemy of great."[2] It's easy to become overwhelmed doing good things, those activities that help others and leverage your gifts. But in saying "yes" to the good, you may preclude the possibility of doing something even more important or significant. Simply saying, "Let me get back to you" rather than saying "yes" may give you the space you need to make this determination.

In many cases, you can say "not me" without saying "no." First chair leaders often delegate to their second chairs the important tasks that they don't want to do or don't have time for. Unfortunately, many second chairs are hesitant to do the same. A willingness to pass the responsibility to another staff member is a great way to say "no" without it being a "no." Like opening the drain on the sink, it keeps you from being overloaded, even as new priorities are coming in. And just as importantly, it develops other leaders and communicates trust in them.

But what about those times when you and the entire team are overloaded, and the new request is a priority from your first chair? Can you say "no" to your boss? In many cases, you can. The best scenario is to sit down with your first chair and review all the different things on your plate. Explain how the new request pushes you well beyond 100 percent, and ask for help with setting priorities or taking something off your plate. Even better, propose a solution that preserves organizational priorities and doesn't burden your first chair. While many second chairs are reluctant to have this conversation, it often has a positive outcome. It's not uncommon for a first chair to remark, "I didn't realize you had so much to do" and then to shift some responsibilities.

Even if the outcome isn't this positive, it is still the right conversation to have. Kevin's first role at the church had been to lead the discipleship program. He did this well, and the combination of his strong leadership gifts and the church's growth led to an expanding list of duties. But even after Kevin became executive pastor, he retained direct responsibility for discipleship. One day in their staff meeting, Kevin's senior pastor said, "I'd like you to take our adult discipleship program to the next level." That prompted Kevin to ask for a meeting with his senior pastor. Kevin presented his case, but he was told that they didn't have funding to hire someone new or anyone on staff to whom these duties could be shifted.

2. Jim Collins, *Good to Great: Why Some Companies Make the Leap… and Others Don't* (New York: HarperCollins Publishers, 2001), 1.

What does saying "no" look like for Kevin and others who feel similarly trapped? Kevin made a conscious decision after that meeting to maintain the current discipleship program rather than trying to expand it. He had explored other options, and none of them seemed feasible. He was confident that the existing program was good (even if it could be improved) and that it supported the church's vision. Kevin realized that he might be seen as not following the directive from his senior pastor, but he wasn't willing for his family or personal life to pay the price that a new initiative would require.

I can't say, "Be like Kevin," because Kevin is a unique person in a unique context. But I can say that second chair leaders often need to say "no" in one way or another, even in respectful or subtle ways to their first chair. And I am confident that getting clear about when to say "no" creates opportunities for you to say "yes" to things that may be life-giving and mission critical.

Saying "Yes"

If saying "no" is a buttress against frustrating role creep, saying "yes" is an intentional step toward greater joy and satisfaction. This can occur in two very different ways. One is to become reengaged with the church or ministry's mission, an idea that will be addressed later in this section. But second chair leaders can also thrive by saying "yes" in small, out-of-the-way corners of their work lives.

Think about it this way. As you reflected on the personal questions earlier in this chapter, did you think of an activity about which you would never say, "I *have* to do this"? This task brings you so much satisfaction that you say, "I *get* to do this. I can't believe I'm paid for doing this." In fact, this task is something you might volunteer to do if it wasn't part of your job. Unfortunately, this is the kind of work that is often squeezed out by role creep. Fortunately, it is within your power to say "yes" to some of these opportunities.

When Dennis was in seminary, his favorite classes were the ones in which he was required to dive deep in God's Word. He loved studying the Bible and after he graduated, he loved teaching Scripture to others. But he found that he had little time for this passion when he moved into an executive pastor role several years later. No one expected Dennis to teach a Bible study class, and he certainly had plenty of other priorities to fill his time. During summer vacation, he visited with an old friend from a previous church. The friend had been a regular in classes that Dennis taught during those years and attributed much of his spiritual growth to what he learned during that season. He was surprised that Dennis wasn't teaching in his current job and encouraged him to find a way to resume this use of his gifts. No one objected when Dennis asked if he could co-lead the men's Bible study for the fall semester. By the end of September, Dennis could already feel his spirit being lifted. When the study concluded just before Thanksgiving, Dennis told his senior pastor that he wanted—actually needed—to continue to find opportunities to teach in order to feed his own soul.

What small things do you need to say "yes" to in order to feed your soul? These aren't the kinds of things that will result in a change in your job description. In fact, they may be so far under the radar that your colleagues won't even know that you're doing them. You may have a gift for counseling and want to engage in this form of ministry for a couple of hours a week. Or you may find a way to mentor one or two of the youth in the after-school program, even though the head of the program is now one of your subordinates.

Sometimes the "yes" is on the radar. It involves taking a leadership role in one of your church or ministry's major new initiatives. This is quite different from stepping in because no one else is available. This is jumping in because it's the perfect intersection between the needs of the organization and your own gifts and passions. This kind of "yes" often grows out of "thinking strategically" (chapter 4) and answering the organizational questions in this chapter. Unlike the previous case, it usually involves a shift in your role and a conversation with your first chair.

Tim's church had launched two campuses, and he had played a vital behind-the-scenes role in both of these success stories. In his second chair role, his team had been responsible for facilities, equipment, administrative support, and ministry coordination. Tim and his senior pastor had jointly selected the campus pastors and had both been involved in mentoring them. In the early stages of planning for the next campus, Tim asked his boss if he could be the campus pastor. At first, the request was met with reluctance. It wasn't due to a lack of confidence from the senior pastor; rather it was because he couldn't imagine not having Tim as a full-time executive pastor. Tim was eventually able to develop a proposal that would allow him to do both, with some of his administrative duties being delegated to others and a strong co-leader being hired for the new campus. The two years that followed were the busiest of Tim's career, but he was often heard telling his colleagues, "I've never felt so alive in ministry."

That's the goal of saying "yes"—to find and embrace those things that can help you come alive and stay vibrant. The "yes" may be little or big in its impact on your duties and the church or ministry, but it's never trivial. That's because the things you do with the right "yes" can extend your shelf life, not incrementally, but exponentially.

Reimagining Fully

If you started with a blank sheet of paper (or new file on your tablet) and described your ideal job, what would you write? What gifts and passions would this job use? What kinds of activities would you spend your time doing?

This is the kind of dreaming that is typically associated with someone who is starting their career or making a major change, or at the very least is planning to leave their current place of employment. But why can't you do it with the intent to reimagine your second chair role while staying in place?

Reimagining can be a powerful exercise for the second chair leader who feels stale and thinks that changing jobs is the only way to get a fresh start. This isn't the feeling that someone has after two or three years. It happens most often after someone has accumulated a number of years of faithful service. That faithful service is the permission point that makes it possible to reimagine.

Faithful, long-tenured second chair leaders have usually established tremendous trust and credibility with their first chairs and within their churches or ministries. They have demonstrated loyalty. They have proven their willingness and ability to tackle tough problems. They have a track record of helping to clarify the vision and then turning it from concept to reality. They are loved and valued.

Imagine that you had this kind of person working for you. Then imagine that he said, "I love being here and being part of this team. I love seeing what God is doing through our ministry. But I'm feeling a little stale. Can we talk about some changes in my role that would reenergize me and give me a new sense of purpose?" Can you imagine saying no to this request? Of course not. You would gladly enter into the conversation with this valued leader. You might see things a little differently than him. You might not agree with everything he requested. You might even offer some helpful insights that hadn't occurred to him. So now put the shoe on the other foot. Don't you think that your first chair would be willing to have this same kind of rich conversation with you?

If this describes you—a long-tenured, faithful, valued second chair leader who is feeling a little stale—then let this be the encouragement that you need to reimagine fully. The second chair leaders I know have great energy and passion. They have no desire to coast into retirement. They've sunk deep roots in their church or ministry and they'd rather not leave. When this is the case, reimagining your role is truly the best option.

Stacy had served in a variety of positions in her church before becoming the executive pastor, but her favorite had been as the pastor for adult discipleship. She continued to oversee that area when she became executive pastor, but with so many other responsibilities, she had little time to be involved in the discipleship ministry. When the church developed a new five-year plan, Stacy was thrilled that discipleship emerged as being central to the strategy. Over the ensuing weeks, Stacy had several meetings with her senior pastor to discuss the practical implications of the renewed emphasis on discipleship, including how it should be staffed. They both concluded that Stacy should step out of the executive pastor role so that she could lead the church's discipleship ministry. She would still be on the executive team and would still be a second chair leader, but with a different title and different focus. To an outsider, Stacy's new role might seem like a step down. To Stacy, it was a reimagined way to thrive in the second chair.

Reimagining may take you down unexpected paths, as it did with Stacy, but that's not all bad. Perhaps "reimagining" isn't even the right word. The best kind of reimagining is a process of discerning the role that God wants you to play. It goes beyond the organizational and personal questions to the most important, spiritual ones. And none of us should be surprised when that journey takes unexpected turns.

As you can see, there are many ways to escape the narrow framing of a "stay or go" decision. Would you be able to extend your shelf life by saying "no," saying "yes," or reimagining fully? That may be all you need to do to thrive again.

Personal Reflection

- Do you feel that you're near the end of your "shelf life"? What factors are contributing to this feeling? Might it be temporary, or have you felt this way for a while?
- If "role creep" is a problem for you, what's contributing to this? In what ways are you part of the problem?
- Review the questions on page 141 and take some time to answer them for yourself.
- What do you need to say "no" to? What do you need to say "yes" to?
- What would your "blank sheet of paper" job look like?

Discuss with Your First Chair

- Discuss any concerns about "role creep" and how these can be addressed.
- Second chairs: Discuss with your first chair any significant areas where you feel the need to say "no" or "yes."
- First chairs: If your second chair is feeling burned out or near the end of his or her shelf life, allow (encourage) time away so that he or she can reflect on changes that would be reenergizing.
- What would a "reinvented" second chair role look like that would serve the church or ministry and extend the shelf life of the second chair?

EPILOGUE

A LETTER AND A PRAYER

Now that you've visited each of the ten springs that can quench your thirst for thriving, what is the next step? Perhaps you already know of one spring that you need to return to immediately. As you read about that practice for thriving, you felt the Holy Spirit nudging you to say, *Pay attention. This is where you need to come to find refreshment and vitality.* If that's the case, then don't let me stand in your way. Run back to that spring as quickly as possible and discover what God has in store for you there. Spend time reflecting on how to apply those principles in your ministry.

On the other hand, you may find yourself drawn toward many of the springs. You may need to make minor adjustments in a variety of areas that will allow you to do ministry in a more life-giving and sustainable way. Or you may realize that much deeper changes are needed in order for you to thrive. Perhaps you feel paralyzed by uncertainty about how to start.

If you can't decide which way to turn, let me suggest that you pause to write a letter and to say a prayer. The letter will be to your first chair, and while I don't know your specific situation, I will suggest some things that you might include. The prayer is a way for you to seek God's wisdom for your next steps and to be reminded of the Holy Spirit's presence in your life.

A Letter

What would you say in a letter to your pastor or executive director (or other first chair) that reflects your desire to thrive? Your letter may be full of gratitude. It may contain some heartfelt frustrations or respectful requests that you've been holding back. You may want to give the letter to your first chair before you begin to work through the discussion questions in this book. Or the letter may simply serve as a way to untangle your thoughts without ever being delivered to your first chair.

Whenever I sit down to write something important, I often stare into space for a while, organizing my ideas and deciding how to start. The questions below may help you get started on your letter:

- What about your first chair and your job are you particularly grateful for? What brings you joy? In what ways are you using your gifts?

- In what ways does your relationship reflect the ideal partnership? In what ways does it fall short? How would you like to grow in this relationship over the coming months?

- How can you best support your first chair? What does he or she most need? Do you have suggestions to ease his or her burdens?

- Has anything happened in the past for which you need to apologize? Perhaps a time when you were disrespectful or weren't as supportive as you should have been? Are you aware of any misperceptions that need to be addressed?

- What frustrations do you need to express to your first chair? How can you do this in a way that is respectful and that focuses on positive changes?

- As you've reflected on the practices of thriving, what organizational changes would you like to propose? These might relate to your role, staff management, systems and processes, governance bodies, or other areas. How does your first chair need to be involved?

- What personal changes—spiritual disciplines, relationships with other second chairs, boundaries—do you need to make in order to thrive? What support do you need from your first chair to make these changes?

- What commitments are you making? Would you like your first chair to help you achieve those commitments and/or hold you accountable?

Whatever you write and whatever you do with the letter, I believe that reflecting and then putting your thoughts into words will be personally meaningful and will help you clarify a path toward thriving.

A Prayer

As with the letter, I don't know what your relationship with God is like or what you specifically need to pray. But I know that it's impossible to thrive without a vibrant spiritual life. Scripture is full of promises, exhortations, and encouragements that can guide a second chair toward thriving. Some of the principles that I find most helpful, along with some of my favorite related verses, are listed below.

- You are a child of God and your heavenly Father loves you deeply (1 John 3:1). This is the most important identity you can have. Be grateful that this ultimate source of thriving can never be taken away from you.

- The honor and rewards that matter most come from God. If you're in a season in which affirmation from people is sparse, lean on promises like those in Psalm 62:7 and Isaiah 49:4.

- When contentment seems impossible, remember Paul's teaching that we can and should be content in all circumstances (Phil 4:11).

- Invite God to search your heart and reveal any sins that are hindering your spiritual vitality and your ministry effectiveness (Ps 139:23-24), knowing that your confession opens the door for God's forgiveness and healing (1 John 1:9).

- As you experience forgiveness, be quick to forgive others who have offended or hurt you (Col 3:13), especially your first chair and others with whom you work closely.

- God has prepared good works for you to do (Eph 2:10), but that work will only be fruitful if you stay connected to the vine (John 15:5). Ask God to reveal how your unique gifts and talents can be used to bear much fruit for the Kingdom.

- Ask God to give you companions who will share the journey with you and help you up when you're down (Eccles 4:9-12).

- As you consider how to apply the practices for thriving, seek God's wisdom on what you should do, remembering the promise and instruction that come with this prayer (James 1:5-6).

What other biblical principles would you add? What is your prayer?

Now that we've explored all ten springs, my hope is that you will truly thrive in the second chair. My prayer is that you will live as the beloved child of God that you are, that the relationship with your first chair will be affirming, that your labors will bear much fruit for the Kingdom, and that you will have great friends to share your joys and struggles with.

> Now to him who is able to do immeasurably more than all we ask or imagine, according to his power that is at work within us, to him be glory in the church and in Christ Jesus throughout all generations, forever and ever! Amen. (Eph 3:20-21)

Appendix A

An Overview of *Leading from the Second Chair*

In *Leading from the Second Chair*, Roger Patterson and I provide an overarching framework for understanding the opportunities and challenges that are unique to this vital leadership role. That understanding begins with a definition. We define a second chair leader as "a person in a subordinate role whose influence with others adds value throughout the entire organization."[1] This definition intentionally omits specific titles or position on an organization chart. Second chair leaders can have a variety of job titles. Sometimes they are clearly in the "number two" role, but this is not always the case. They may be one of several people on a senior leadership team (often with other "second chair leaders").

Central to this definition is the idea of organization-wide influence. Second chair leaders see the big picture. Regardless of their specific role or responsibilities, they think globally about what is best for their church or ministry. And they use their influence, in concert with the first chair, to work toward that end.

This kind of influence is important because a first chair (senior pastor, executive director, bishop, and so on) can't provide all of the leadership that a church or ministry needs. If the first chair leader is the only person exercising leadership gifts, then that organization is guaranteed to fall short of its God-given potential. Effective second chair leadership is essential for creating and maintaining forward movement in any church or ministry.

So what is "effective second chair leadership"? *Leading from the Second Chair* answer this question by describing three apparent paradoxes: subordinate-leader,

1. Mike Bonem and Roger Patterson, *Leading from the Second Chair: Serving Your Church, Fulfilling Your Role, and Realizing Your Dreams* (San Francisco: Jossey-Bass, 2005), 2.

deep-wide, and contentment-dreaming. They are "apparent" paradoxes because the best second chair leaders don't settle for either/or thinking but strive for both/and. Even though this will stretch them, they realize that it is the only way to lead well from the second chair.

The *subordinate-leader* paradox focuses on the relationship between the first and second chair leaders. Those in the second chair know they are in a subordinate role. They may not like using this term, but the reality is that they report to someone who is their boss. They know that insubordination is wrong and that it can wreak havoc within the ministry. Yet they also know that a leader doesn't simply wait to be told what to do. Leaders have ideas of their own. They take initiative. They push to make changes that will address problems or expand the Kingdom impact of the ministry. In doing these things—in leading—they will occasionally get ahead of the person in the first chair. Both/and thinking pushes second chairs to wrestle with how to be loyal subordinates while at the same time using their influence and leadership gifts to advance the mission.

The *deep-wide* paradox recognizes that second chair leaders need to both master a myriad of details and think about the big picture. In many organizations, the second chair serves alongside a visionary first chair. Part of the value that the second chair brings is an ability to think about all the moving parts that must be in place in order to accomplish a high-level vision. In addition, they may have direct responsibility for one or more ministry areas. A second chair who doesn't excel in these "deep" duties will not last long. By the same token, the second chair leader who only sees the details will also struggle. Adding value *throughout the organization* requires the ability to think "wide." Some second chairs are wired in such a way that deep comes easily, while others naturally gravitate toward the big picture. Few master this paradox without intentional effort.

The *contentment-dreaming* paradox forces a second chair leader to ask: "Can I be content today while continuing to dream about tomorrow?" In good seasons, contentment comes easily. But even in difficult circumstances, contentment is possible for the second chair who realizes that there is Kingdom work to do and personal lessons to learn. It's a belief that God is still present and that seasons come and go. Some second chairs begin to believe that dreaming is the exclusive domain of first chair leaders, and they slip into complacency as their dreams slowly fade. Others insist on realizing their dreams immediately and become demanding and abrasive. Those who live in the both/and of contentment and dreaming give their best efforts in the present and trust that a God-given dream will come true in God's time.

Understanding and mastering these three apparent paradoxes is important for anyone who wants to be an effective second chair leader. In the decade since *Leading from the Second Chair* was published, I've learned that effectiveness is important, but it's not enough. That's why I've written this new resource to help second chair leaders thrive.

Appendix B

A First Chair's Guide to Thriving

Let me start this appendix by stating a couple of assumptions that I'm making about you. You're in a first chair role—senior pastor of a church, executive director of a non-profit ministry, bishop or denominational head. Someone (or more than one person) you truly care about supports you and the ministry in a "second chair" role. He or she has read this book and wants to discuss it with you. You may not have time to read a book about second chair leadership, but you do have time for your second chair. You want this person to thrive, not only for his or her well-being, but also because a thriving second chair increases your own ability to thrive and the organization's potential to soar.

Let me also make a few assumptions about that second chair leader. He or she has already demonstrated initiative by reading this book and asking to meet with you. He knows that you hold one of the keys for thriving, which is why he wants to meet. He genuinely cares about you and this church or ministry. That's important, because if he has some weighty matters to discuss, he does so with good intentions.

So what will be on your second chair's agenda? Her relationship with you will almost certainly be one of the topics. That's what the first three chapters of this book focus on. If there are points of tension between you, she knows that these must be resolved. If she senses that you don't fully trust her, she will want to know what missteps she has made and how she can rebuild that trust.

Trust is important in any relationship, but it's especially important between first and second chairs. When they are at their best, they are working toward a partnership, which I define as "a commitment to sharing directional leadership that is based on a common vision, an appreciation for each other's complementary gifts, and a high level of trust that develops over time." Do you want this kind of partnership with your second chair? Does this definition point toward steps you need to take?

Trust is also the foundation that will allow you to give honest feedback to each other. Every leader has flaws. Every leader has blind spots. Only some leaders are actively working to overcome these weaknesses. Your second chair wants to become a better leader, and you're in the best position to help him see where he needs to improve. Will you give him the benefit of a frank and caring evaluation that will help him grow into his potential?

In the same way, your second chair has a unique perspective on the areas where you need to grow as a leader. Because she works closely with you, she is well aware of the gaps in your skills and how these impact the church or ministry. Because she cares about you and the organization, the observations she wants to offer are intended for good, not for harm. The question is whether you're willing to receive this feedback. If you are, then make this process feel less risky by inviting your second chair to be honest with you.

A final aspect of the first-second chair relationship is role clarity. You may think that the expectations for the second chair role are crystal clear, but don't be surprised if your second chair thinks otherwise. He knows that the role will always be dynamic, changing with the needs of the organization. When he is confused or overloaded or frustrated, he needs to be able to discuss this with you. Today's clarification about the extent of his authority or what you rank as the highest priority paves the way for tomorrow's success rather than conflict.

The middle four chapters address a variety of responsibilities that are typical in second chair roles: planning for the future, managing staff, developing processes and systems, and interacting with governance bodies and committees. This list may be a reminder of why you have someone serving in a second chair role. You may not want to be bothered with these details, but the reality is that you cast a long shadow from your first chair position. Your second chair will probably recommend changes in one or more of these areas, but she will want your support before proceeding. Few things are more frustrating for a second chair than a first chair who "doesn't want to bother with the details" and then routinely second guesses or reverses a decision in the eleventh hour.

The final three chapters challenge your second chair leader on a more personal level. I've encouraged him to change how he thinks about success and to grow in his dependence on God. I've recognized the loneliness of this job and emphasized the value of deep relationships with other second chair leaders. If he's feeling stagnant, I've suggested that he look for ways to extend his shelf life by reinventing his role. You may think that these personal matters don't concern you, but you have a part to play. You should listen as he talks about the changes he plans to make. You can gently challenge him if you think he needs to do more or applaud him for stretching himself. You can hold him accountable for commitments that he has made. And you can celebrate with him when he succeeds.

As you can see, your second chair may have a lot that he or she wants to discuss. I hope that you will be open to this conversation. In *Good to Great*, Jim Collins describes one model of leadership that he calls "a genius with a thousand helpers."[1] That's what happens when a first chair leader has all the great ideas and just needs a lot of "helpers" to implement those ideas. The problem, according to Collins, is that this style doesn't produce a great organization.

First chairs who don't invest in developing their second chair leaders are essentially saying, "I just want to be surrounded by 'helpers.'" The best first chairs, however, know they're not the smartest people in the room. They know they need other leaders, not helpers, so that their churches or ministries can achieve their God-given potential. My hope and prayer is that you and your second chair will each become better leaders as you engage in this rich conversation about thriving.

1. Jim Collins, *Good to Great: Why Some Companies Make the Leap... and Others Don't* (New York: HarperCollins, 2001), 45.

APPENDIX C

ADDITIONAL RESOURCES TO ORGANIZE SELECTIVELY

Chapter 6 addresses the processes and systems that can improve the effectiveness of a church or ministry. Because the topic is so extensive, this appendix lists some additional resources that can help you go deeper on various subjects.

Resources That Relate to Multiple Subjects

- The Church Network (formerly National Association of Church Business Administrators), www.TheChurchNetwork.com. A variety of written resources, webinars, and annual conference.
- XPastor, www.XPastor.org. White papers and articles, executive pastor certification program, and annual conference.
- Christian Leadership Alliance, www.ChristianLeadershipAlliance.org. Articles, training programs, and annual conference.
- *In Pursuit of Great AND Godly Leadership: Tapping the Wisdom of the World for the Kingdom of God* by Mike Bonem (Jossey-Bass, 2012)

Metrics and Goals

- *Doing the Math of Mission: Fruits, Faithfulness and Metrics* by Gil Rendle (Rowman & Littlefield, 2014)

- *Missional Renaissance: Changing the Scorecard for the Church* by Reggie McNeal (Jossey-Bass, 2009)
- *Keeping Score: How to Know If Your Church Is Winning* by Dave Ferguson (Exponential Resources, 2014)
- *Good to Great and the Social Sectors: A Monograph to Accompany Good to Great* by Jim Collins (HarperCollins, 2005)

Staff Management and Human Resources

- *Amplified Leadership: 5 Practices to Establish Influence, Build People, and Impact Others for a Lifetime* by Dan Reiland (Charisma House, 2012)
- *When Moses Meets Aaron: Staffing and Supervision in Large Congregations* by Gil Rendle and Susan Beaumont (Rowman & Littlefield, 2007)
- MinistryPay, www.MinistryPay.com. Comparative salary information for ministry positions.
- *2016–17 Compensation Handbook for Church Staff* by Richard R. Hammar (Church & Clergy Tax, 2015)
- Best Christian Workplaces Institute, www.BCWInstitute.com. Offers a staff engagement survey and related services.

Legal

- Church Law and Tax, www.ChurchLawandTax.com, Richard Hammar, senior editor, offers two print or electronic newsletters.

CPSIA information can be obtained
at www.ICGtesting.com
Printed in the USA
LVOW01s1251080816
499485LV00002B/2/P